B
U
P

**Virginia Stagni**

# DREAMERS WHO DO

Intrapreneurship and Innovation
in the Media World

Foreword by
**Antonio Calabrò**

Afterword by
**Tony Haile**

*Cover*: Cristina Bernasconi, Milan
*Typesetting*: Laura Panigara, Cesano Boscone (MI)

Copyright © 2021 Bocconi University Press
EGEA S.p.A.

EGEA S.p.A.
Via Salasco, 5 - 20136 Milano
Tel. 02/5836.5751 – Fax 02/5836.5753
egea.edizioni@unibocconi.it – www.egeaeditore.it

First edition: October 2021

| ISBN Domestic Edition | 978-88-99902-77-3 |
| ISBN Digital Domestic Edition | 978-88-238-8323-9 |
| ISBN International Edition | 978-88-31322-28-7 |
| ISBN Digital International Edition | 978-88-31322-45-4 |

*To my parents*
*To the dreamers who do*

# Contents

# Foreword

The complex but nonetheless virtuous relationships between information, liberal democracy and the market economy have been a crucial focus of the political and economic literature of the last three centuries. Today, the radical technological changes of the digital world and the internet, as well as those seen in the geopolitical sphere (the end of the bipolar balance of power between the USA and the USSR after the fall of the Berlin Wall and the implosion of the Soviet empire, the rapid pace of globalisation, and the sudden emergence of new international players), have subjected the media world to continual, overwhelming stress testing. The world of information has been shattered by these changes. However, we still have a real need for high-quality journalism, to reconfirm and reintroduce the values of political and economic democracy that we have no intention of discarding.

The challenge, then, is to try to hold together these values, which remain anchored in civic consciousness, above all in the countries of the West, with economic and social transformations prompted by high-tech innovation – and so to hold together democratic tradition and digital innovation in order to ensure a future for high-quality information.

It is against this contextual backdrop that Virginia Stagni's work is so valuable. It reconstructs the history and context of the development of information, partly through the effective use of an educated knowledge of literature and philosophy (references to Plato and the "Allegory of the cave" at the beginning are particularly relevant). It prompts critical reflection on the productive and cultural processes of journalism. And it offers an in-depth analysis of the choices we need to make to tackle the questions posed by "creative destruction" and "disruptive" innovation, in terms of both the news context and media business models, with new synergies between journalists, marketing and technology. The author's direct experience with the *Financial Times*, one of the world's most authoritative newspaper groups, provides significant support for her advanced strategic ideas, which suggest a new balance between moral values and corporate production dynamics.

This brings us to the first important point to consider. To express it in the words of a maxim well known in the offices of the *Financial Times*: "Our newsroom needs to be data-informed and not data-led". The information available to readers – or, more accurately, users – of the news, and the extraordinary processing power offered by artificial intelligence algorithms, allow journalists and their editors to understand their audience ever more deeply, and this can shape the choices they make in their news products. But allowing yourself to be guided exclusively by social media likes, or thinking that reach is the only measure of success, is to court trouble. Stagni cites the pertinent warning of Nobel laureate Herbert A. Simon: "A wealth of information creates a poverty of attention". The background noise generated by everything circulating on the web hinders a real, in-depth understanding of essential news. The "perceptual deception" of Plato's cave has an up-to-date parallel in our own confused and contentious times.

Good journalism, if it is to combat this "perceptual deception", must therefore maintain a dialectical relationship with its public to an even greater extent than in the past. It is responsible for continuing to follow its own principles: providing thorough and reliable information; refining the tools that allow readers to understand events; and developing up-to-date interpretative keys to political, economic and social changes.

Staying with the classic paradigms of high-quality information in the English-speaking world, we should recall and be guided by the slogan of the *New York Times*, "All the news that's fit to print", and that of the *Washington Post*, "Democracy dies in darkness". Aside from their communicative power in American rhetoric (Hollywood's depiction of journalism has contributed to the myth-making too), these are professional and ethical prescriptions relevant to Europe's media world.

What of Italian journalism? In its recent history, it has produced exemplary work in reporting, investigation and comment. Even today, at a time when the fundamentals of liberal democracy and the market economy are in crisis, and in the face of extraordinarily strong competition from powerful authoritarians, the construction of an Italian "public discourse" – in the sense of the principles laid out by a theorist such as

Jürgen Habermas – urgently calls for a relaunch through relationships between high-quality news and the values of citizenship and democratic participation.

And here is the second central point to consider and reconstruct, in terms of both the news and business models. "Values over volume should be the common mantra", Stagni rightly claims, criticising the obsession with Twitter and Facebook likes (beloved of populist and nationalist politicians) and insisting on the value of engagement, not the number of hits, as the guiding criterion for journalism. Volume-led editorial models are likely to remain profitable in the near term, but they will eventually mean abandoning the capacity for critical thought and depending wholly on volatile followers. This state of affairs, moreover, is one widely affected by the growing dissemination of fake news, which is strongly political in character (here again appears the shadow of the anti-democratic manoeuvrings of autocratic and totalitarian powers).

The response to this invests responsibility in the world of journalism (an unrelenting campaign to educate readers in the importance of fact checking is needed), but also in the work of democratic political organisations, social actors and leading cultural figures. Crucial, also, is a general increase in levels of education, as well as a widespread awareness of the risks of disinformation, in order to tackle fake news on the broad topics of the environment, health and science. In this sense, our dramatic times of pandemic and recession offer valuable food for thought. As we know, given the goals of sustainable development, defined by the UN, supported by Pope Francis and documented in leading economic and international social literature, we have a critical need for high-quality information.

The third point to consider in Stagni's book concerns the renewal of business models for journalism; a different approach must be taken if they are to continue to be "trustworthy entities". "A new entrepreneurial mindset" is needed. Better still, news companies need "intrapreneurs" – alert, curious, irreverent innovators who accelerate the diffusion of innovation into established company procedures. These are intrapreneurs understood as "corporate entrepreneurs". The book contains much fascinating material on how to navigate traditional hierarchies and ideas for creative disruption. More generally, it is worth bringing to mind our need for figures capable of synergising and synthesising different values and spheres of knowledge – philosophical engineers or (why not?) poetic engineers: individuals capable of constructing a "polytechnic culture" in which the humanities and scientific knowledge are hybridised into a new and original mindset incorporating different worlds, from business to training, from research to politics itself. Italy, with its "culture of polytechnic enterprise", is a master of this – from Pirelli to the public companies of the 1950s, via "Machine Civilisation" and Olivetti. The country can continue to offer fascinating inspiration.

"Collaboration is the key to innovation", Stagni claims, and with good reason. As she says, "What matters is to be a driven human. People who drive change, drive others, drive the future".

The renewal of the journalism sector should be guided by the human factor. Women have a special role in this – their presence in the sector is growing, even if, unfortunately, not with all the recognition, in terms of roles and value, that they deserve. This is another goal to reinforce and complete – though with the awareness that innovation is a continual process: it is non-linear and imperfect, but essential to implement. It is worth recalling Karl Popper's teaching on science: this is a process that progresses via trial and error, discovery and fresh starts.

What is on the horizon, then? The answer is a new Enlightenment of empathy, in which the intellect engages positively our emotional intelligence. And a new digital humanism. This involves working for a better, more knowledgeable future and the "knowledge economy". The reassuring conclusion is that this is the future, despite conflict and controversy, which we are already walking towards.

*Antonio Calabrò*

# Introduction

Born into a wealthy and noble family, Plato was studying for a career in politics when the trial of Socrates took place. It was 399 BC. Inspired by the philosopher, Plato abandoned plans for a political career and turned to philosophy, following his mentor, Socrates. He then opened a school (known as the Academy) in Athens, dedicated to the Socratic search for wisdom.

The myths narrated by Plato in Book VII of his best-known work, *The Republic* (gr. Πολιτεία; lat. Res publica), certainly has a tangible value for the education of any man and woman who considers themselves to be human.

The Allegory of the Cave is expressed as a conversation between Socrates and Glaucon. The philosopher describes a scenario where a group of people live in a cave-like dwelling. They are chained to the wall so that all they can see is the wall in front of them. The objects that apparently move in front of them are just shadows: they have been projected onto the wall thanks to the lighting of a fire burning from a side of the cave not visible to the chained slaves. So, they are not real objects but are simulacra of statuettes, puppets. The noises the slaves hear belong to the shadows as well. The truth is that the noises, the puppets and the fire are made by artists who lead the entire dwelling, so that the slaves live in a complete illusion. Plato says that only a philosopher can discover the truth and free his mind from this fantasy. The rest of the prisoners are destined to live at the bottom of the cave forever.

However, if a slave were able to free himself and could gradually explore the cave and then leave it and observe the external reality, if he once returned to the cave and told what he knew and saw, he would not be believed by others, but indeed attacked and killed. Similarly, the philosopher who rises from the level of opinion and belief (from the simulacra of things) to a vision of reality at its highest intelligible level (in mythological terms, looking at the light of the Sun) and then divulges his knowledge, such a philosopher would not be believed by those who are still enslaved by their passions and opinions. Indeed, the philosopher would be considered insane and killed (as happened to Socrates).

What you have read is one of the most successful metaphors in the history of universal thought.[1]

A dark cave becomes the representation of our universe, while the external world represents the place of ideas (Hyperuranium), of reality, of truth, where the sun of knowledge shines. The captive slaves, on the other hand, are men. The chains, ignorance. The images on the bottom, the perceptions of the senses. A state of unconscious submission, of which the path to liberation is only one: philosophy and its liberating actions such as thinking, logos (=word), critical perspective and dialogue.

And this is what we will humbly try to represent dynamically within this book. We will try to understand the steps to get out of the dark cave we might find ourselves immersed in when approaching the 'news' realm. Thus begins a minimal (the topic is too vast!) but hopefully engaging journey that attempts to walk the path of better understanding the chaotic and cacophonic news ecosystem, how to approach a variety of stimuli, how to turn into a critical thinker and how to build a career in one of the most exciting and challenging industries – the media.

If, with the advent of modern man, there is an awareness of the relativity of knowledge and the values that guide our society, increasingly hyperbolically magnified by that crisis loudly shouted in every media, we are increasingly inclined to live in a state of rarefied indifference, the realm of the impossibility of making a decision. And the web is a perfect

---

[1] This allegory has been used by many other artists and authors to represent the fictional reality men are constrained to view and live in. Two examples to stimulate your curiosity. Kubrick, in the film *Clockwork Orange*, gives the protagonist the "Ludovico cure": he is forced to watch projections for hours on end. As if chained in the cave, he can only look at the images in front of him, with his eyes wide open and his body in a straitjacket. In the Wachowskis' Matrix trilogy, the 20th-century human race believes that it lives freely in the world but, rather, it is controlled by machines that keep humans imprisoned. The movies suggest that not all humans will be willing to abandon their 'cave' when discovering the truth: they would favour the peace and safety of their illusory life. The parallelism with Plato's story is even more explicit in the film's last scene: the protagonist looks directly at the sun, as does the captive freed from the cave.

sea in which to get lost and forget about this difficult circumstance in which we constantly wander.

But this lack of control comes from a fallacious if not non-existent management and enhancement of knowledge: we increasingly believe it is a synonym of power and control rather than a path of freedom and speech.

If the approach to communication methods has become increasingly global, disassembled and disintermediate, a metamorphosis of productive and cultural processes within the news has been formed. Therefore, a rethinking of the founding values of journalism as a social entity and democracy's bastion is urgently needed, in which the primary objective is still shared living and living well.

*Figure*   Plato's cave

Illustration by Leonardo Malaguti

## Πολιτεία, VII Book (514 b – 520 a), Plato

[Socrates] And now, I said, let me show in a figure how far our nature is enlightened or unenlightened: – Behold! human beings living in a underground cave, which has a mouth open towards the light and reaching all along the cave; here they have been from their childhood, and have their legs and necks chained so that they cannot move, and can only see before them, being prevented by the chains from turning round their heads. Above and behind them a fire is blazing at a distance, and between the fire and the prisoners there is a raised way; and you will see, if you look, a low wall built along the way, like the screen which marionette players have in front of them, over which they show the puppets.

[Glaucon] I see.

[Socrates] And do you see, I said, men passing along the wall carrying all sorts of vessels, and statues and figures of animals made of wood and stone and various materials, which appear over the wall? Some of them are talking, others silent.

[Glaucon] You have shown me a strange image, and they are strange prisoners.

[Socrates] Like ourselves, I replied; and they see only their own shadows, or the shadows of one another, which the fire throws on the opposite wall of the cave?

[Glaucon] True, he said; how could they see anything but the shadows if they were never allowed to move their heads?

[Socrates] And of the objects which are being carried in like manner they would only see the shadows?

[Glaucon] Yes, he said.

[Socrates] And if they were able to converse with one another, would they not suppose that they were naming what was actually before them?

[Glaucon] Very true.

[Socrates] And suppose further that the prison had an echo which came from the other side, would they not be sure to fancy when one of the passers-by spoke that the voice which they heard came from the passing shadow?

[Glaucon] No question, he replied.

[Socrates] To them, I said, the truth would be literally nothing but the shadows of the images.

[Glaucon] That is certain.

[Socrates] And now look again and see what will naturally follow if the prisoners are released and disabused of their error. At first, when any of them is liberated and compelled suddenly to stand up and turn his neck round and walk and look towards the light, he will suffer sharp pains; the glare will distress him, and he will be unable to see the realities of which in his former state he had seen the shadows; and then conceive someone saying to him, that what he saw before was an illusion, but that now, when he is approaching nearer to being and his eye is turned towards more real existence, he has a clearer vision, what will be his reply? And you may further imagine that his instructor is pointing to the objects as they pass and requiring him to name them, -will he not be perplexed? Will he not fancy that the shadows which he formerly saw are truer than the objects which are now shown to him?

[Glaucon] Far truer.

[Socrates] And if he is compelled to look straight at the light, will he not have a pain in his eyes which will make him turn away to take and take in the objects of vision which he can see, and which he will conceive to be in reality clearer than the things which are now being shown to him?

[Glaucon] True, he now.

[Socrates] And suppose once more, that he is reluctantly dragged up a steep and rugged ascent, and held fast until he's forced into the presence of the sun himself, is he not likely to be pained and irritated? When he approaches the light his eyes will be dazzled, and he will not be able to see anything at all of what are now called realities.

[Glaucon] Not all in a moment, he said.

[Socrates] He will require to grow accustomed to the sight of the upper world. And first he will see the shadows best, next the reflections of men and other objects in the water, and then the objects themselves; then he will gaze upon the light of the moon and the stars and the spangled heaven; and he will see the sky and the stars by night better than the sun or the light of the sun by day?

[Glaucon] Certainly.

[Socrates] Last of he will be able to see the sun, and not mere reflections of him in the water, but he will see him in his own proper place, and not in another; and he will contemplate him as he is.

[Glaucon] Certainly.

[Socrates] He will then proceed to argue that this is he who gives the season and the years, and is the guardian of all that is in the visible world, and in a certain way the cause of all things which he and his fellows have been accustomed to behold?

[Glaucon] Clearly, he said, he would first see the sun and then reason about him.

[Socrates] And when he remembered his old habitation, and the wisdom of the cave and his fellow-prisoners, do you not suppose that he would felicitate himself on the change, and pity them?

[Glaucon] Certainly, he would.

[Socrates] And if they were in the habit of conferring honours among themselves on those who were quickest to observe the passing shadows and to remark which of them went before, and which followed after, and which were together; and who were therefore best able to draw conclusions as to the future, do you think that he would care for such honours and glories, or envy the possessors of them? Would he not say with Homer, *"Better to be the poor servant of a poor master"*, and to endure anything, rather than think as they do and live after their manner?

[Glaucon] Yes, he said, I think that he would rather suffer anything than entertain these false notions and live in this miserable manner.

[Socrates] Imagine once more, I said, such an one coming suddenly out of the sun to be replaced in his old situation; would he not be certain to have his eyes full of darkness?

[Glaucon] To be sure, he said.

[Socrates] And if there were a contest, and he had to compete in measuring the shadows with the prisoners who had never moved out of the cave, while his sight was still weak, and before his eyes had become steady (and the time which would be needed to acquire this new habit of sight might be very considerable) would he not be ridiculous? Men would say of him that up he went and down he came without his eyes; and that it was better not even to think of ascending; and if anyone tried to loose another and lead him up to the light, let them only catch the offender, and they would put him to death.

[Glaucon] No question, he said.

[Socrates] This entire allegory, I said, you may now append, dear Glaucon, to the previous argument; the prison-house is the world of sight, the light of the fire is the sun, and you will not misapprehend me if you interpret the journey upwards to be the ascent of the soul into the intellectual world according to my poor belief, which, at your desire, I have expressed whether rightly or wrongly God knows. But, whether true or false, my opinion is that in the world of knowledge the idea of good appears last of all, and is seen only with an effort; and, when seen, is also inferred to be the universal author of all things beautiful and right, parent of light and of the lord of light in this visible world, and the immediate source of reason and truth in the intellectual; and that this is the power upon which he who would act rationally, either in public or private life must have his eye fixed.

[Glaucon] I agree, he said, as far as I am able to understand you.

[Socrates] Moreover, I said, you must not wonder that those who attain to this beatific vision are unwilling to descend to human affairs; for their souls are ever hastening into the upper world where they desire to dwell; which desire of theirs is very natural, if our allegory may be trusted.

[Glaucon] Yes, very natural.

[Socrates] And is there anything surprising in one who passes from divine contemplations to the evil state of man, misbehaving himself in a ridiculous manner; if, while his eyes are blinking and before he has become accustomed to the surrounding darkness, he is compelled to fight in courts of law, or in other places, about the images or the shadows of images of justice, and is endeavoring to meet the conceptions of those who have never yet seen absolute justice?

[Glaucon] Anything but surprising, he replied.

[Socrates] Anyone who has common sense will remember that the bewilderments of the eyes are of two kinds, and arise from two causes, either from coming out of the light or from going into the light, which is true of the mind's eye, quite as much as of the bodily eye; and he who remembers this when he sees any one whose vision is perplexed and weak, will not be too ready to laugh; he will first ask whether that soul of man has come out of the brighter light, and is unable to see because unaccustomed to the dark, or having turned from darkness to the day is dazzled by excess of light. And he will count the one happy in his condition and state of being, and he will pity the other; or, if he have [*sic*] a mind to laugh at the soul which comes from below into the light, there will be more reason in this than in the laugh which greets him who returns from above out of the light into the cave.

[Glaucon] That, he said, is a very just distinction.

[Socrates] But then, if I am right, certain professors of education must be wrong when they say that they can put a knowledge into the soul which was not there before, like sight into blind eyes.

[Glaucon] They undoubtedly say this, he replied.

[Socrates] Whereas, our argument shows that the power and capacity of learning exists in the soul already; and that just as the eye was unable to turn from darkness to light without the whole body, so too the instrument of knowledge can only by the movement of the whole soul be turned from the world of becoming into that of being, and learn by degrees to endure the sight of being, and of the brightest and best of being, or in other words, of the good.

[Glaucon] Very true.

[Socrates] And must there not be some art which will effect conversion in the easiest and quickest manner; not implanting the faculty of sight, for that exists already, but has been turned in the wrong direction, and is looking away from the truth?

[Glaucon] Yes, he said, such an art may be presumed.

[Socrates] And whereas the other so-called virtues of the soul seem to be akin to bodily qualities, for even when they are not originally innate they can be implanted later by habit and exercise, the of wisdom more than anything else contains a divine element which always remains, and by this conversion is rendered useful and profitable; or, on the other hand, hurtful and useless. Did you never observe the narrow intelligence flashing from the keen eye of a clever rogue – how eager he is, how clearly his paltry soul sees the way to his end; he is the reverse of blind, but his keen eyesight is forced into the service of evil, and he is mischievous in proportion to his cleverness.

[Glaucon] Very true, he said.

[Socrates] But what if there had been a circumcision of such natures in the days of their youth; and they had been severed from those sensual pleasures, such as eating and drinking, which, like leaden weights, were attached to them at their birth, and which drag them down and turn the vision of their souls upon the things that are below – if, I say, they had been released from these impediments and turned in the opposite direction, the very same faculty in them would have seen the truth as keenly as they see what their eyes are turned to now.

[Glaucon] Very likely.

[Socrates] Yes, I said; and there is another thing which is likely. or rather a necessary inference from what has preceded, that neither the uneducated and uninformed of the truth, nor yet those who never make an end of their education, will be able ministers of State; not the former, because they have no single aim of duty which is the rule of all their actions, private as well as public; nor the latter, because they will not act at all except upon compulsion, fancying that they are already dwelling apart in the islands of the blest.

[Glaucon] Very true, he replied.

[Socrates] Then, I said, the business of us who are the founders of the State will be to compel the best minds to attain that knowledge which we have already shown to be the greatest of all they must continue to ascend until they arrive at the good; but when they have ascended and seen enough we must not allow them to do as they do now.

[Glaucon] What do you mean?

[Socrates] **I mean that they remain in the upper world: but this must not be allowed; they must be made to descend again among the prisoners in the cave, and partake of their labors and honors, whether they are worth having or not.**

[Glaucon] But is not this unjust? he said; ought we to give them a worse life, when they might have a better?

[Socrates] You have again forgotten, my friend, I said, the intention of the legislator, who did not aim at making any one class in the State happy above the rest; the happiness was to be in the whole State, and he held the citizens together by persuasion and necessity, making them benefactors of the State, and therefore benefactors of one another; to this end he created them, not to please themselves, but to be his instruments in binding up the State.

[Glaucon] True, he said, I had forgotten.

[Socrates] Observe, Glaucon, that there will be no injustice in compelling our philosophers to have a care and providence of others; we shall explain to them that in other States, men of their class are not obliged to share in the toils of politics: and this is reasonable, for they grow up at their own sweet will, and the government would rather not have them. Being self-taught, they cannot be expected to show any gratitude for a culture which they have never received. But we have brought you into the world to be rulers of the hive, kings of yourselves and of the other citizens, and have educated you far better and more perfectly than they have been educated, and you are better able to share in the double duty. **Wherefore each of you, when his turn comes, must go down to the general underground abode, and get the habit of seeing in the dark. When you have acquired the habit, you will see ten thousand times better than the inhabitants of the cave, and you will know what the several images are, and what they represent, because you have seen the beautiful and just and good in their truth.** And thus our State which is also yours will be a reality, and not a dream only, and will be administered in a spirit unlike that of other States, in which men fight with one another about shadows only and are distracted in the struggle for power, which in their eyes is a great good. Whereas the truth is that the State in which the rulers are most reluctant to govern is always the best and most quietly governed, and the State in which they are most eager, the worst.

[Glaucon] Quite true, he replied.

[Socrates] And will our pupils, when they hear this, refuse to take their turn at the toils of State, when they are allowed to spend the greater part of their time with one another in the heavenly light?

[Glaucon] Impossible, he answered; for they are just men, and the commands which we impose upon them are just; there can be no doubt that every one of them will take office as a stern necessity, and not after the fashion of our present rulers of State.

[Socrates] Yes, my friend, I said; and there lies the point. You must contrive for your future rulers another and a better life than that of a ruler, and then you may have a well-ordered State; for only in the State which offers this, will they rule who are truly rich, not in silver and gold, but in virtue and wisdom, which are the true blessings of life. Whereas if they go to the administration of public affairs, poor and hungering after their own private advantage, thinking that hence they are to snatch the chief good, order there can never be; for they will be fighting about office, and the civil and domestic broils which thus arise will be the ruin of the rulers themselves and of the whole State.

[Glaucon] Most true, he replied.

[Socrates] And the only life which looks down upon the life of political ambition is that of true philosophy. Do you know of any other?

[Glaucon] Indeed, I do not, he said.

[Socrates] And those who govern ought not to be lovers of the task? For, if they are, there will be rival lovers, and they will fight.

[Glaucon] No question.

[Socrates] **Who then are those whom we shall compel to be guardians? Surely they will be the men who are wisest about affairs of State, and by whom the State is best administered, and who at the same time have other honors and another and a better life than that of politics?**

[Glaucon] They are the men, and I will choose them, he replied.

[Socrates] And now shall we consider in what way such guardians will be produced, and how they are to be brought from darkness to light, – as some are said to have ascended from the world below to the gods?

[Glaucon] By all means, he replied.

[Socrates] **The process, I said, is not the turning over of an oyster-shell, but the turning round of a soul passing from a day which is little better than night to the true day of being, that is, the ascent from below, which we affirm to be true philosophy?**

[Glaucon] Quite so.[2]

---

[2] This selection is taken from the Benjamin Jowett translation, available at gutenberg.org. The original text is Plato's Πολιτεία, VII Book (514 b – 520 a).

# Part I.
## Journalism is the first draft of history

# 1    Janus

"Study the past if you would define the future"
*Confucius*

One of the most overrated concepts of our age, and yet intrinsically connected to modern life, is *disruption*. Derived from Latin (*dis-* 'apart' + *rumpere* 'to break'), it means tearing something into pieces, destroying it completely. As an institutionalised entity that produces and disseminates facts, information and reference-points for the public (Schudson, 2008) and makes the sense of modern life (Hartley, 2008), journalism must deal with this phenomenon. Embracing it with openness means changing to avoid being left behind.

These days, journalism is living through a crisis and a revolution of historic proportions. Journalists are not working on a newspaper; they are working in the news (Quinn, 2005) – meaning that the industrial logic that dominated the mass media ecosystem for decades is gone, and they cannot rely on it any more. Kovach and Rosenstiel (2001) stated that the press survival depends on journalists' ability to communicate what it is and why, their *raison d'être*. Recalling the theory of disruption elaborated by Clayton M. Christensen, it is necessary to "find something that the medium can do really well, its 'job to be done'".

Journalism does need democracy to exist and everyone agrees that democracy does need journalism. Now more than ever, we need it as an institution that makes sense of this disrupted and chaotic scenario and analyses the world's most challenging transformations. Actually, to evaluate the diverse expressions of different individual and group perspectives that effectively represent the model of today's 'complex democracy', segmented media and general media is required. Finding the right balance between these two is the key to describing the disruptive world we live in.

Journalism is at a crucial turning point. Of course, it has to look back to defend its historical, predominant position, but it also needs a long-term vision to thrive in the future. To do this, new profiles, hybrid figures with different and varied skill sets, are essential.

In ancient Roman times, Janus was the God of beginnings and passages, divinity of change and time. He had two faces: one that looked to the past, the other one that observed the future. Janus presided over the beginning and end of conflicts.

Janus is, to me, the best representation of journalism's essence today. This allegory will accompany us through our journey in this book.

*Figure 1*    Janus

PIECE OF SCULPTURE, PROBABLY INTENDED TO REPRESENT
THE GOD JANUS
Photographed by Sommer and Son, Naples

The first duality is a duality of ontology.

Journalism needs to reflect on what it stands for, what its values are (defined by its past) and be simultaneously ready to understand and adapt to the future by staying relevant, without losing or forgetting its legacy.

The second duality is its organisational structure.

As with all cultural organisations, the control of a news outlet is split between two entities: the creative part (the editorial thinkers, the newsroom) and the business part. The balance between the two is to be handled with extreme caution. In fact, the interests of the commercial side of the organisation do not always match the editorial ones. This is why the need for hybrid roles, which understand the wants and needs of both sides – especially when you add another player into the game, technology – has never been more needed.

The third and last duality is its market dynamics.

The news outlets are media platforms that operate in a 'two-sided market': they have to watch and please two groups of customers, readers and advertisers – both sources of sustainability for the business model of news.

Complex, right? But so fascinating!

Let's look at the business model to clarify why journalism needs to evolve constantly while being an equilibrist.

The main goal of the so-called newspapers (or 'news entities') is to produce content that will attract users' eyeballs (more traditionally, we would say readers' attention). Economically, the aim is to balance network externalities between readers (users) and advertisers, both sources of revenues.

The business model is still the same, though: publishers sell 'attractive' content to audiences and spaces to advertisers, and they charge them a price. There are then two possible scenarios: people are directly charged for the content (as in a subscription business model) or they are indirectly charged through the attention they pay to the advertisement spaces (in a 'free' business model – where it is evident there is nothing for free...).

These two revenue streams are mutually dependent: when circulation increases, advertising rates do too, generating bigger revenues; when audience attention drops, the rates fall too, as do revenues. Different business models arise depending on the different rates of 'power' these two revenue engines have.

As a tightrope walker, news outlets have a tough job controlling so many different market dynamics and players – even just looking at themselves.

The situation gets more complex when we look at the competitors' landscape as well, and generally at the media context, which has intrinsically changed over the past two decades. In fact, what journalism is facing can be defined as a cultural clash (Thurnam, 2008), a reshaping of the overall information infrastructure of news (gathering, distribution, selling) and the role of journalism as a social entity.

You may ask: why this book? To analyse all these different dynamics and to offer a human factor solution to the complex ecosystem that journalism plays within.

# 2   The smell of ink and a misfit journey

"That's the press, baby!"
*Humphrey Bogart in Richard Brooks' movie,* Deadline U.S.A. (1952)

I was born surrounded by the smell of ink. In my teenage years, while studying classics at high school, I used to help at my parents' small press agency every morning before going to school. They worked on press services, mostly creating press releases for Italian companies – mainly enterprises from my hometown, Bologna. For my parents and, consequently, for me, this meant reading all the national and local newspapers and magazines every morning. My dad used to stop every dawn, at 5 am, at the newsstand and come back to the car with two shopping bags full of papers. There were more than 150 news titles. As most of them were hot off the press, having access to freshly printed newspapers meant nurturing curiosity and hunger (and also a certain sense of exclusivity, as we were the first to get the news!). However, this also meant my hands turning black by the end of the reading time and my dad's car – plus my nostrils – being flooded with the smell of ink. I have always associated these memories with the idea of getting my hands dirty, of living the experience not only with my brain but also with my body, immersing myself in it. That period of my life undoubtedly shaped my approach to my future studies and job.

Once in Milan, I did not take journalism as my field of studies (even if storytelling has always been my true passion), but I tried to carve my niche between news and business. I remember that, at that time, one thing was clear in my head. There is a sweet spot in the news industry, especially in studying and understanding how crucial cultural change is within the media ecosystem and in exploring business modelling and interactions through technologies and social media. At Bocconi University, where I studied Economics and Management for the arts, culture and communication (thanks to my family who decided to get a meaningful loan to give me this opportunity), I took some majors in publishing and political communication, finally realising how powerful the media can be in shaping society and citizens' perceptions and opinions. Therefore, I decided to explore the field of sociology. So I moved to London and, thanks to a scholarship, attended the London School of Economics and Political Science, where I took a Master of Science in Media and Communications (I chose a one-year programme as I really needed to start working to help my parents to repay the loan!).

During those years, I studied media as an expression of social life and a means for social change, and the social causes and consequences of human behaviour within the media ecosystem. I loved investigating the structure of groups, organisations and societies within the media space and how people, both individuals and audiences, interact within these contexts.

That is how I found an interesting spot between the social sciences and economics aspects of the news. I discovered I was very interested in figuring out which business model can contribute to quality and informative journalism. From that moment on, I had a critical question that turned into a personal mission. *How can we save quality journalism in the digital age?*

I founded a small media business, *Revolart*, a magazine dedicated to arts and culture that could be a practical space where I could apply all the models I had studied in Milan. We started as a group of close friends, and turned it into a true newsroom ecosystem. Imagine more than 50 students in Milan and others who were travelling worldwide for their Erasmus programmes writing reportage that told their stories and recounted their experiences within the art scene. After this experience, I was aware that the part of the job I preferred was 'behind the scenes', managing media and communication. It was 2012, and we were only at the beginning of the social media era.

When I started to write my Master's thesis, I was advised to talk to various practitioners and insiders to get a real sense of the news world out there. Only a very few of them replied to my many emails and LinkedIn messages and agreed to be interviewed. But surprisingly, four people from the *Guardian*, the *Economist* and the *Financial Times* invited me to visit their company. All of them agreed through LinkedIn messages (showing how valuable social networks can be if used effectively).

For the FT, Jon Slade, Chief Commercial Officer, invited me for a chat: the person I least expected to answer my message – because of his seniority and how busy someone in his role must be – actually invited me to visit the FT. Talking with him was not just an incredible moment for someone like me who was (and is) so passionate about journalism (I entered the FT building for the first time – and to me that was a dream coming true) – but also genuinely enlightening, a once in a lifetime opportunity. In such a senior corporate leader, I found an enthusiastic, passionate visionary thinker, the sort of person I always aspired to be in the future – if I ever entered the corporate world as an employee (and not a start-up founder). More than anything, I was shocked to find an inclusive door opener: I mean that it was clear that Slade understood his social role, not just the shining title that he held in the boardroom. He could play an impactful role in opening the doors of an organisation such as the FT to the next generation of readers and leaders directly and innovatively. And he was doing this pragmatically and quickly, asking for feedback, experiences, thoughts on the future of the news industry, valuing a (stranger's) opinion – and very open to being challenged. His actions and way of approaching others, with emotional intelligence, made a news entity (considered by most of us an 'untouchable' place and authority) receptive and open to dialogue with new minds from diverse backgrounds.

I believe my interest and passion for the news industry was quite evident while chatting to Mr Slade. He suggested I should get in contact after graduation to share my dissertation. However, I always thought the opportunity would end with that meeting and a few emails, for the sake of my LSE thesis.

Six months after that meeting, Slade received my dissertation and unexpectedly got back to me via email, suggesting I should think about the FT as a reachable, possible place where I could start my career – helping to bring change in the news industry. I did so. Under his guidance, I evaluated the open positions that the company could offer to someone with my profile and background. I would have never perceived the FT as a place for me: I was not yet a specialist, I did not want to be a journalist and I thought the business side of the company could have been explored only after a long time working at consulting firms – in order to have the credibility to work on new business models and partnerships.

After many interviews (and some big NOs!) and exploring different opportunities, I finally obtained the role of programme coordinator in a small start-up owned by the FT group, the Corporate Learning Alliance (now Headspring), which is where everything started. This role, as an assistant of many managers, was extremely beneficial for my managerial profile: I learnt to be overtly organised, to manage external providers and to be an expert in logistics and programme management, from flight bookings to catering choices. All these tasks turned out to be as useful as the things learned during my university part-time jobs in Milan, such as waitress, babysitter, school tutor...

It was, honestly, one of the most uncertain moments of my life. I felt the pressure of living in one of the world's most exciting but scary cities, London – and following my passion, the news industry, while turning down way more financially comfortable opportunities in the consulting world. I followed my gut, and thought that if I needed to spend 70% of my days working, I would choose to spend it on something I was passionate about – and where I could see a change-maker impact was needed (and tangible). It was not an easy choice to make in one of the most expensive cities in the world, and with a huge burden (my loan), and I still remember spending my nights asking myself if the path I was on was honestly the right one.

But it was in those circumstances, immersed in so many questions and overthinking moments – and also engaged on a lot of tasks in my coordinator job I did not feel the best fit for – I got an idea for a project, FT Talent Challenge, and decided to get to the bottom of it.

Impactful projects need sponsors, as an artist or an explorer needs a wealthy patron. Even in the contemporary corporate world you need champions at top-management level. I found mine in Jon Slade, who, as I have said, shared an inclusive vision for journalism with me. I prepared a pitch, put all my effort into it and presented it to the FT's CCO and then the CEO.

The project got positive feedback and I was offered a fixed-term contract to make the Challenge happen. A six-month 'trial' opportunity while leaving a full-time job in an executive education start-up? Sometimes life gives us risky trade-offs; but, I knew, once again, I was following a vision and my desire for impact – which would lead me to the Business Development Manager role I have now. I needed to deliver results based on defined KPIs, there were corporate and bureaucratic hurdles – and I needed to convince other FTers to be part of the journey. I took this as a challenge, and I enjoyed it profoundly. Thankfully, I had an incredible manager, Kayode Josiah, who helped me navigate areas I did not know about, network internally (I did not know anyone in the business as I was coming from an FT spin-off) and a board sponsor who dealt with and for me with some persuasive actions (read politics). They believed in the idea as much as I did – and they wanted to see it tested and implemented. Therefore, I was given the tools to play the corporate game fairly.

A fact should be considered. My role did not exist within the company when I first began. While evaluating all the possible positions for me on the job market, I had the unpleasant feeling of being a misfit in most of them, and that idea is still present at the back of my mind. Looking at other careers, I often felt discouraged and not on a clear track. I was Italian, I did not have a British accent (actually I had a very strong Italian one!) or a cultured spoken language. I had studied many things with passion and perseverance, but had not followed a traditional academic path to get into the news. But in some ways my 'peculiarity' was my strength, and I knew that I had to find a way to demonstrate this: to carve my niche as a free mind inside the company. I had the chance to meet bosses who would understand my nature and bet on me.

That is how I became what I like to call an *intrapreneur*. Through this book, I want to show you how you can turn into one and how to make an asset of your misfit feelings – and to pragmatically approach your future.

However, let's go back to the news world and see what is happening in the media context – and what an intrapreneur can do in it.

# 3    Disruption of the (media) market

"We all live under the same sky, but we don't all have the same horizon"
*Konrad Adenauer*

Nowadays, media companies face tough competition to obtain consumers' attention and become profitable. Therefore, they need to continuously innovate to remain relevant and competitive in the ferocious run to the future.

Over the past 15 years, many companies have closed, and the number of journalists has been cut in half. According to data from the US Bureau of Labor Statistics' Occupational Employment Statistics, 37,900 people worked as reporters, editors, photographers or film and video editors in the American newspaper industry in 2018. This was down 14% from 2015 and 47% from 2004.[1]

Many consider 2005 to be the highest point for newspaper profitability in the UK, thanks to a prosperous economy and cheap printing costs owing to automation. Besides, broadband connection and the 'web mindset' were still not wide enough spread to bring about proper change.

But in the United Kingdom, 33 local newspapers closed between 1 January 2019 and 19 August 2020, according to a Press Gazette analysis. Of them, 13 closed after Covid-19 hit the UK. Since 2005, 265 local newspapers have disappeared in the UK. How could this happen?

---

[1] Read the full report on the Pew Research website: https://www.pewresearch.org/fact-tank/2020/04/20/u-s-newsroom-employment-has-dropped-by-a-quarter-since-2008/; and use the interactive graphs here: https://www.journalism.org/fact-sheet/newspapers/.

*Figure 2*   Employment in newspaper newsrooms

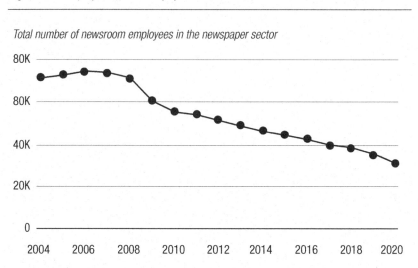

*Total number of newsroom employees in the newspaper sector*

*Note*: The OEWS survey is designed to produce estimates by combining data collected over a three-year period. Newsroom employees include news analysts, reporters and journalists; editors; photographers; and television, video, and film camera operators and editors.

*Source*: Pew Research Center analysis of Bureau of Labor Statistics Occupational Employment and Wage Statistics data.

You may think that the answer is logical and obvious, like any other market dynamic: news is not in demand any more. But let's think of the problem more holistically.

This is not just a media ecosystem issue: 88% of Fortune 500 companies in 1955 were no longer extant in 2015, having been acquired, merged, (mostly) gone bankrupt or being no longer significant (Perry, 2014). A 2019 McKinsey's study calculated that the average life expectancy of Standard & Poor's 500 companies was circa 35 years in 1980. It is estimated that it will be 12 years by 2027. The same study believes that by 2027, 75% of the brands quoted today on the S&P 500 will have vanished. Companies can and do disappear, and the same is true for news organisations.

We are assisting in the process of creative destruction in action. Schumpeter wrote in 1942 that *creative destruction* (a term he coined) is the disassembling of established practices to make space for innovation, a "process of industrial mutation that incessantly revolutionises the economic structure from within, incessantly destroying the old one, incessantly creating a new one".[2] Now more than ever, this phenomenon is proliferating – in the media ecosystem as much as in other sectors. The Internet is the symbol of creative destruction, encompassing different industries, expertise and ecologies.

In more recent days, London Business School professor Julian Birkinshaw said that disruption is an "external force shaking up the status quo. Brexit is a disruption; a volcano erupting in Iceland and shutting down European airspace is a disruption; blockchain is a disruption." Simple and straightforward. As suggested in an *Economist* article by Terri Williams,[3] when such events happen it is "a David-versus-Goliath scenario in which large, successful companies make the mistake of thinking what got them to the top will keep them there. They don't just underestimate the competition – they don't understand the battlefield."

Another reason for this destruction lies in complexity: the bigger the company, the more complex it is to manage, therefore becoming more vulnerable – as a lot of energy is invested in keeping it together (Garelli, 2016).

According to Garelli, a valid comparison is with thermodynamics. First, we should consider the significance of energy, which is the capacity to do work intended as a movement or a change. All the energy is transferred from an object, or a system, to another during the work. If no energy enters the system, there could be a spread of potential energy, and this loss is irreversible. This is entropy, according to the second law of thermodynamics – a physical measure for uncertainty and randomness. The larger the system is, the more external energy will be needed to keep it in equilibrium at the end of the process.

By analogy, Garelli says that this is what makes large companies die because they need more and more energy in terms of management to survive. The bigger they are, the more energy they need.

Am I suggesting that small is better? Or perhaps that we need to accept that the 'too big to fail' principle is no longer valid in the digital era? The answer is too multifaceted to be categorical. Indeed, I believe that the complexity of larger and digital companies, which need to invest their manage-

---

[2] Joseph Schumpeter, *Capitalism, Socialism and Democracy*, p. 83 (Routledge Classics, 1950).

[3] Read the full article "Be a Disruptor to Avoid Disruption" here: https://execed.economist.com/blog/industry-trends/be-disruptor-avoid-disruption.

ment energies on so many levels and in so many ecosystems (with no space and time limits), are not comparable with the organisations of 20 years ago.

And so, what?

If disruption and innovation shorten the average company lifespan, this means that changes in strategies and organisational models, and new role models for the leadership of a new era are required not only for their survival, but also for their thriving.

Fortunately, companies can count on an already existing and strongly adaptive resource, their employees. Within a never previously seen flexible way of living our work life (thanks also to the technological sprint occurring during Covid-19), employees and a solid company culture that embraces change as a new positive challenge are the primary assets for a healthy long-living company.

And here is where the intrapreneur role comes out. To be drivers of innovation from within, to be disruptors and not the disrupted,[4] corporations need to integrate an entrepreneurial mindset into the DNA of their established organisations, developing intrapreneurship.

*Avoid being disrupted by creating a culture of disruption* – this is the mantra, and this is what corporate entrepreneurs have to do. Instead, intrapreneurship – sometimes overlooked as a cowardly form of entrepreneurship – needs to become a part of company culture. Only by integrating intrapreneurship as a shared and common attitude will organisations keep visionary thinkers within the company, while growing and innovating continually in terms of the corporation, its culture, its products and, above all, its competitiveness.

This exploration of a new entrepreneurial mindset can hopefully be helpful for both the employer and new younger talent. Even if you are not leading a start-up, you might have a calling to create a disruptive company that is aligned to the complexity of the contemporary age, or for being an impactful employee, someone whose roles, responsibilities, and actions can have an impact on their company but, above all, outside them.

In whichever case, these pages are for you.

---

[4] I highly recommend the paper by D. Skok, C. Christensen and J. Allworth, "Breaking News, Be the Disruptor", *Nieman Foundation for Journalism*, Harvard University School (2012). This article made me realise my interest in this field and I completely fell in love with the subject of disruption and journalism. I have to say that it was thanks to this paper I chose this career.

# 4    The topos of the intrapreneur

"The Macintosh team was what is commonly known as intrapreneurship: a group of people going, in essence, back to the garage, but in a large company"
*Steve Jobs*, Newsweek (1985)

The study of etymology is a prolific – and yet surprisingly quick – way to understand the history of human minds, practices and social behaviour. That is why, back in my high school days, I loved studying Latin and Greek, and I took classical studies (the nerdy but cool course!). Knowing words and their efficacy means knowing the world and its evolutions.

From a pure etymological perspective, *intrapreneur* comes from *intra-* 'within' (the company) + a shortened form of 'entrepreneur'. I am going to consider this word first.

Within British culture, the term 'adventurer' was often used as a synonym. Actually, from the mid-16th century, 'entrepreneur' was used in English and French to describe a person who behaves actively, a person who acts. It comes from the French *'entreprendre'*, to 'undertake', that originates from the Latin "*inter prehendere*", "to seize with the hand", as physically working on, and mastering something. Literally, getting your hands dirty. Does that ring a bell?

During the 18th century 'entrepreneur' entered economic theory (Richard Cantillon, in his "Essai sur la Nature du Commerce en Général" was the first), as a person who creates a business and takes risks, with a willingness to deal with uncertainty. Do you remember the definition of entropy given above?

Intrapreneur is a very young term. Sustainable business school founder Gifford Pinchot III coined the term in 1978 and defined it as "dreamers who do". Intrapreneurs are employees who do for corporations what an entrepreneur does for his or her company or start-up. Being innovators, they act as owners when they approach their projects, taking "hands-on responsibility for creating innovation of any kind, within a business".

Pinchot's theory is all about "you do not need to leave a corporation to become an entrepreneur", and thanks to my career, I couldn't agree more.

I would rather consider myself an *intrapreneur* (or *corporate entrepreneur*) with a "getting your hands dirty" role, rather than an entrepreneur according to the usual definition.

I like to compare it with the process of reading a newspaper in the "old way", which I told you about at the beginning of this book. Therefore, I always have the image of my dirty fingers and the smell of ink in mind when I think of an entrepreneurial job.

Intrapreneurs have entrepreneurship at their core because entrepreneurship is an attitude, not a skill. It is a calling, as many entrepreneurs define it, and a passion-driven risk-taking adventure – as the etymology shows. It is not a job or a career description; it is more of an artistic attitude about a creative vision and experiential approach to work and, generally, life. It's about taking risks, with resilience, while creating something new, a new business in most cases.

On Pinchot's website,[1] we can find the ten commandments for intrapreneurs. I am going to reproduce it here for your own interpretation and inspiration.

1. Come to work each day willing to be fired.
2. Circumvent any orders aimed at stopping your dream.
3. Do any job needed to make your project work, regardless of your job description.
4. Find people to help you.
5. Follow your intuition about the people you choose, and work only with the best.
6. Work underground as long as you can – publicity triggers corporate immune mechanism.
7. Never bet on a race unless you are running it.
8. Remember it is easier to ask for forgiveness than for permission.
9. Be true to your goals, but be realistic about the ways to achieve them.
10. Honor your sponsors.

---

[1] https://www.pinchot.com/2011/11/the-intrapreneurs-ten-commandments.html.

However, intrapreneurs are very different from entrepreneurs.

Intrapreneurs decide to work for a company, while entrepreneurs fund one. Intrapreneurs take career-related risks, as they do not worry when it comes to big monthly payroll risks if they make a bad decision, the opposite of entrepreneurs.

Therefore, company dynamics are quite different for intrapreneurs, who need to be agile and play around in an already existing ecosystem, with its rules and forces.

I chose to start my career within a big company because I wanted to learn more about the corporate world from the inside and from a well-established company. I think it is valuable to adapt to and learn a stated and defined corporate culture, and to understand the personal dynamics and the key leadership skills that managers and entrepreneurs need when they act within large teams, as part of huge departments or as part of an organigram, "the company".

While entrepreneurs create their company culture, intrapreneurs adapt and maybe disrupt part of that culture.

This is a true and real challenge, and I find it exciting as it needs a completely different mindset. It means being able to act within a defined space – where sometimes your win values double. For instance, you can change something both internally and externally with a disruptive project that changes at the same time the way the company does something and also has an external impact on customers' perception of it.

The value of intrapreneurship and the intrapreneur's adventure is, to me, a unique working life experience – and it is exactly what I want to share in this book.

# 5    Chaos theory and Network Journalism: every era has the kind of journalism that it deserves

"The only things certain and unchanging facing the newspaper industry in the future are uncertainty and change"
*Hernandez* (1996:9)[1]

Let's start from the beginning.

In this a-temporal, hyperlinked, cacophonic liquid modernity, networked journalism is the form that is blossoming. Nowadays, it appears as a hybrid of professional journalism and bottom-up content creation, a mixed process that uses new platforms and technologies combined with traditional practices. Based on a context of uncertainty and unpredictability, where different economic and cultural dynamics are performing, this disruptive digital scenario has reshaped the entire ecosystem in which journalism used to play.

This transformation is partially due to the changes in the system's infrastructure, which moved from mass media to a network media, and partly because of changes in technologies that are enabling different actors to interplay in all the stages of the news value chain.

The Earth's crust is made of plates whose movement is called tectonic shift. The results of this phenomenon can be, for example, earthquakes or eruptions. A tectonic shift, a radical change, in the media has two main effects – changes in news consumption and changes in news creation. Changes in news consumption are about the coming to fruition through multiple platforms and devices of a different de-ritualised and atomised practice that is based on the user as a singular individual; this requires new strategies to engage with a specific audience. Changes in

---

[1] In Pablo J. Boczkowski, *Digitizing the News: Innovation in Online Newspapers*, p. 65 (MIT Press, 2004).

news creation stand for a wholly altered value chain, from the gathering to the distribution to the selling of news, with new actors within it (e.g. readers, aggregators, social platforms, influencers, activists) who are working with the new logic of the network.

Adapting to this context has become the main challenge for any news incumbent,[2] first defining their role for and within society (its semantics), and secondly, taking an economic perspective, in finding a new sustainable infrastructure.

So, how are quality journalism producers reacting to this changing environment? If there is a general "assumption that journalism will continue to exist" as Professor of Media, Communications and Social Theory Nick Couldry used to say in his LSE classes, how is this economically possible?

Finding the answers to these questions seems like discovering the Holy Grail, and everyone in the news field (practitioners and academics) is struggling to find a final answer.

The ambiguous ecology that I will describe below is the first indicator of what news practitioners have to face and how challenging (but exciting) working in the news world can be.

### The Black Swan in San Francisco

> πάντα χωρεῖ καὶ οὐδὲν μένει
> "Everything changes and nothing stands still"
> *Heraclitus*

News. Many of you may connect the word with papers, laptops, tablets or smartphones, even if the last are options that only appeared a few years

---

[2] Incumbent – as seen on Investopedia (2021): "An incumbent in business most commonly refers to a leader in the industry. While it may normally refer to a person, that isn't always the case. It can also be used to describe a company or a product as well. A company may, for instance, possess the largest market share or may have additional sway within the industry. As such, incumbents in an industry may change in response to changes in the market. For example, Blackberry producer Research in Motion was once considered an incumbent of the smartphone market in 2007. During the fourth quarter of 2014, Apple, the producer of the iPhone, replaced it as the incumbent based on worldwide sales." https://www.investopedia.com/terms/i/incumbent.asp

ago. We have witnessed a transition in this short time from a culture dominated by television and physical papers to one that is dominated by digital devices. It sounds unbelievable that something considered now so essential as the smartphone – a sort of appendix to our fingers and brains – has been changing the media for less than ten years. Moreover, unique structural changes have been happening: on these new information distribution channels, never previously witnessed volumes of eyeballs are available for monetisation and attention; furthermore, algorithms, not journalists, decide and optimise what people read, listen to and watch. It sounds like a stirring opportunity for news brands and their businesses. However, it is impossible to wonder how quality journalism can continue to thrive in the contemporary media ecosystem in which newly emerging tech giants are disrupting the old news business models and customer relationship.

Let's take a step back and take a holistic approach to the ecology of the 2000s.

At the beginning of the 2000s, we witnessed the rise of new platforms, habits and communication methods. In the last two decades we have seen some milestones: Facebook 2004, Twitter 2006, iPhone 2007. The milestone, game-changing event of those years was, unquestionably, the 2007 MacWorld Conference & Expo in San Francisco.

We can call this, especially the iPhone discovery, the *Black Swan* moment for media and communication, to use the words of Nassim Nicholas Taleb, sociologist and philosopher.[3]

How did the business of newspapers react to these changes, these Black Swans? How did journalists and news production, the news value chain, adapt to the new technologies?

"Uncertainty is the name of the game at this stage"
*Molina* (1997:224)

When researching this field, I came across a fascinating theory representing the context we are talking about – the "chaos theory" of Brian

---

[3] According to Taleb, a Black Swan is an event with three specific characteristics. First, it is an isolated event, which could not be predicted in the past, second it has a gigantic impact. And, last, but not least, the human mind is naturally pushed to find reasons for its advent. His book is highly recommended: *The Black Swan: The Impact of the Highly Improbable* (Penguin Books, 2007).

McNair (2005, 2006). Taking a broad view of society, he outlined a networked communication system with a "cultural chaos" as its fundamental structure, in which people "have access to more information than ever before" (2006:199) and the information flux runs at a new speed, stimulated by new digital tools.

This cultural clash disassembled the old communication system and infrastructure and journalism as a social entity.

As outlined, the news world's old mass media linear structure as we knew it is dead.

*Figure 3*    Sender – Recipient

---

# SENDER → RECIPIENT

---

Until a few decades ago, we had one-way communication: a few senders, an oligopoly of media outlets that we can classify as the only centres and hearts of information that were used to centralise news gathering and distribution. They transmitted a message – not tailored or personalised, but a single and unique one – to THE audience, thought as one mass receiver. Made at specific times of the day, this one-way line of communication (the audience expected not to respond) turned into a ritual. It was the Hegelian morning prayer, that memento of the day dedicated to reading one newspaper of reference in a well-defined moment of mass audience life. The morning news on paper, the dinner-time TV news show; communication happened in well-known and defined moments through a unique, direct line of messaging – and providing a unique one.

Thanks to game-changing tools such as the personal computer and then the iPhone, this structure was replaced by a "space of flows" – to use Castells' words (1996).[4] It is made of flexible and decentralised communication strings, part of the global cybernetic space. The exposure of humans to this flux is constant and untouched by any space or temporal constraints.

David M. Ryfe, who studied how American newsrooms cope with innovation, efficiently sums up the context by saying that "invented as a

---

[4] Manuel Castells, *The Rise of the Network Society* (Blackwell, 1996).

*Figure 4*   Network

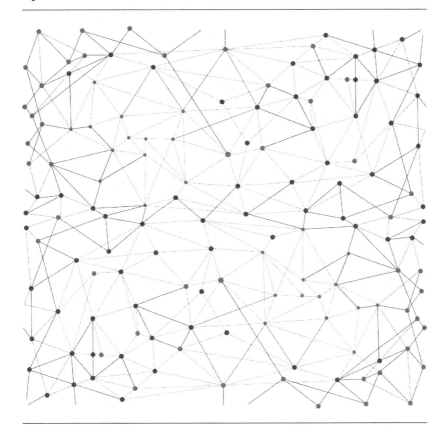

mass medium, and native to a mass society, journalism is migrating, in
fits and starts, to a networked medium"[5].

With the surge of a networked media structure, the relationship between news and readers completely changed. Readers – or, better, users
(we will understand soon why we must change the terminology) have
access to an unlimited amount of information whose constantly active
flux is moving at a new speed, stimulated by new digital technologies and
tools. These fluxes are communication spaces, decentralised ropes going
from one side to the other. Imagine a spider's web where there is not one

---

[5] David M. Ryfe, *Can Journalism Survive? An Inside Look at the American Newsroom* (Polity Press, 2012).

central nuclear origin but nodes, as Castells wrote. All these nodes are disseminators (different news entities) positioned in a space without time and limits. Any user can produce news and information can be a node (even an Instagram user, a social media user). The reliability of the node depends on the number of others it is connected to. More nodes means more information distribution and reach, more influence and relevance within this network space (the spider's web).

Ansgard Heinrich (2011:31), who explored journalistic practice in interactive spheres when outlining a deep study of networked journalism, writes that the old journalistic organisations are now repositioned in this structure and have become nodes located within this global information flow, becoming "information nodes". However, this repositioning for traditional journalism infrastructure was "not [an] easy step to take" (ibid.): the network ecosystem is made of unpredictability and uncertainty, and the chaos paradigm that McNair depicted with his theory forecasted a "turbulent, unpredictable, extreme" news culture (ibid.) to play in.

Journalism is now a disintegrated, a-temporal, unspaced product and multiple-sided communication. It is an open process, accessible to other information producers: readers or, to be precise, users.

### From reader to user

Beforehand, in the mass media structure, the (mass) audience had a precise way to use the information (as a reader, if the message was on paper, for instance, it was to read), and it was identified as 'the readership'. Now, network users have multiple ways to access the information and experience it (reading the content, listening to it on a podcast, watching it via video, etc.). Moreover, they have multiple ways of interacting – sharing, commenting, copying, quoting, 'unfollowing' it – so that similar content doesn't appear any more on a 'feed', the new atemporal space of news discovery and encountering.

Therefore, 'reader', 'readership' and 'audience' are not any more the best way to identify the 'users', the active individuals who absorb the contents and interact with them.

Being able to realise the complexity of this system and manage these spaces is pretty tricky. In an industry known for being resistant to change, this is a considerable challenge. However, as digital disruption approached the journalism system, investments were required at news organisation level. From the editorial staff's news gathering process to the marketing team's methodology, the entire system had to cope with running technologies. This shift took and is taking time, work and training, and consequently resources.

Ensuring the business model's sustainability is vital for journalism's survival.

### The disrupted news value chain

To understand the significant challenges for news organisations in the past two decades, let's try to understand what happened to the news value chain.

One historic change that the news industry has seen since the 2000s revolutions relies on news distribution. In the past, news publishers did not know their readers. Think about it. How could news publishers get in touch with their readers and have a sense of their preferences, understanding, tastes? The newspaper industry survived for decades, not knowing anything about its readers, habits, likes and wishes. A few letters from a restricted number of 'fans' to the newspaper's editor were the only way to connect with the readership directly. Customer feedback was rarely used. Otherwise, the newsstand was the only place where a genuine connection with the reader happened. Its owner knew readers' habits (for instance, when they were getting the paper to read it), their demographics (their 'profiles'), their preferences. This happened because, in the linear mass media structure, a close relationship with the readers was not needed.

The digitalisation of the news industry changed everything. Suddenly, we had the opportunity to build a first and direct relationship with our readers and customers, just as the newsstand used to. The development of a digital offer switched the mass media logic – and therefore the network system – irreversibly changing the news distribution and, hence, the news–audience(s) relationship.

Publishers now distribute their products through the newsstand and different platforms. In addition, they use other formats that allow them to spread the news 24/7. They have a direct relationship with users through constant and definable contact, most of the time enabled by data, and publishers need to leverage that.

"Data has been the largest catalyst of *Financial Times*'s digital growth", former FT Chief Data Officer Tom Betts used to say. If handled properly, they give a complete understanding of the users, allow customer-centric business and projects, and make the news business profitable, even in the current ecosystem.

However, atomising contents on multiple platforms for volume reach rather than thinking with revenue-driven logics (and value strategies) is a significant risk for many publishers.

Now, the gravitational centre, the 'king of the newsroom', is the user. Being audience-centric and designing strategies for customers and consumers is therefore the key, the game-changing approach.

Publishers did not have this knowledge before. Knowing data is an incredible advantage but also a complex new ecology to play with. In fact, in the 20-year window that led to the emergence of a cacophonic network system, many new agents have entered the formerly unique relationship with the readers. New platforms, devices, actors (social media and search engines) took over that relationship, and algorithms instead of editors and publishers own the news distribution chain.

There is also an enormous quantity of information floating around that can only lead to a scarcity of attention.

It is impossible to describe all the multiple transformations occurring in the field fully: individually and together, the disruptions that journalism is facing are fascinating. But, as Ryfe writes (2012:138), "focusing too strictly on any one of them risks missing the forest for the trees". In general, this system challenged the entire mindset of the news 'industry' (if we can still call it that, with its controversial problems (and costs). It presents opportunities in terms of quality, differentiation and contents but also drawbacks. Moreover, the new players, online sources, aggregators, search engines and social networks, are active complements to and competitors for legacy media regarding trust and audiences.

As the specialists of information economies Shapiro and Varian (1998) outline, the industrial economy logic in the mass media was driven by economies of scale. The economics of networks drives the new information economy. Networks have a fundamentally different economic characteristic, and the value of connecting to a network depends on the number of other (loyal) people already connected to it: the bigger and the more specialised, the better.

## "A wealth of information creates a poverty of attention"

The Internet, giving a great abundance of contents, turns attention into a scarce resource. Previously, in a mass media environment, the information was short and packaging it in the form of an "attention trap" was the newspaper business. Then, this attention was sold to advertisers (Currah, 2009). Now, in the networked age, as the Nobel prize winner Herbert A. Simon (1970) said, "a wealth of information creates a poverty of attention" and consequently a scarcity of revenues from the advertisers (increasing the economic value of attention) and therefore changing the revenue stream structure of the news industry forever, to a subscription-based model and an advertisement-based one.[6] The network structure turned the news from a standard generalised product, into a customisable, personalised, specialised one, with significant effects on the content and the advertising business.

As Joseph Turow's (1997–2011) studies show, this niche specialisation of the advertising industry turns the attention of revenue seekers to the data of these customer-specific groups, making the newspaper lose its value as a large-scale medium and so a mass attractor. The value (read, profitability) is in the niche and consequently in the network system hands, not in the news outlets. This means that advertisement is not a substantial subsidy for the news anymore.

## Multiplatform and multi-format

The physical product has been replaced by many physically and virtually unbounded spin-offs from newsroom activity (articles, videos, apps, podcasts, etc.), spread through different network spheres without any geographical boundaries or a short shelf life. Deadlines and time constraints were at the base of journalism until the 20th century. Now

---

[6] "...in an information-rich world, the wealth of information means a dearth of something else: a scarcity of whatever it is that information consumes. What information consumes is rather obvious: it consumes the attention of its recipients. Hence a wealth of information creates a poverty of attention and a need to allocate that attention efficiently among the overabundance of information sources that might consume it." Herbert Simon, *Designing Organizations for an Information-Rich World* (Johns Hopkins Press, 1971).

time acquires a new 'regime of flow'. As Barnhurst (2011: 98-123) outlines, digital brought an "unbound, unlimited product with variable production cycles" (the content is a-temporal, archive-able, editable and updatable), diffused on many other platforms. This new timing and 24/7 accessibility of the news brings, from a reader perspective, a de-ritualisation of the information consumption – news is now constantly in a person's individual daily life. Tech innovations allow the news experience to be no longer a Hegelian morning prayer but as something that is constantly there, in the flux of our life, at breakfast, during lunch, in the toilet... The information momentum is often interpreted by users (and here the etymology of the word efficiently expresses the epistemology of the word itself, 'to use') as a 'consultation action'. For a singular piece of required information, a sort of 'atomised content', the news provider is questioned and not experienced as a discovery practice.

For sure, this 'news cyclone' supports a political and social disruption of the controlled public sphere of the mass media age; however, this constant unframed space leads to a floating information overload that is impossible to follow and brings about many problems.

The network ecosystem tends to have no strict editorial guides or sources. Moreover, if the network enables a "mutualised journalism", to quote Rusbridger (2009), open to collaboration between different actors, Cass Sunstein (2001) argues on the other hand that there is a hidden closeness to the net. Individuals tend to cluster with like-minded others, as in real life, generating polarisation, echo-chamber and filter-bubble effects. Following the Daily Me prediction of Nicholas Negroponte (1995), many news outlets now offer digital self-targeted news, bringing the fragmentation of the audience's content to the scene. According to Johanna Vehkoo (2010:31), the newspaper represented a "bundle of information" that forced the reader to see and interact with different visions and also with unexpected content. Sunstein sees, in the collapse of these "general-interest intermediaries" (newspapers), the disappearance of the "shared experience" (standardised) newspaper represented among the readers (essentially the citizens). This has consequences in terms of the democratic aims of the news organisation as an institution as "common experiences made possible by the media provide a form of social glue" (2001:6). With the new personalisation trend, this social gathering facilitator is challenged.

The problem now is finding a "relationship between the news and the rhythms of a networked society" (Ryfe, 2012:145). Finding the balance between opportunities to seize and threats to overcome is the main task for practitioners and analysts of disruptive networked journalism.

In this context, news organisations have to ask themselves not just where to find new forms of subsidy but how the public sphere can be forged in this new environment. In its normative arguments for "reconstructing journalism's public rationale", it is necessary, as Cloudry outlines, for journalism to convince practitioners, advertisers and, above all, users, of its importance.

Indeed, the sense-making function of journalism becomes even more significant in the complex network context. Journalism and its features such as filtering, communicating and distributing valuable quality information on the right platform at the right moment are now more than ever required to bring order to this information chaos. Therefore, the competitive advantage of legacy players as trustworthy reference points in society can turn into a valuable asset. Only professional editors, correspondents, producers have the time, the capabilities and the resources to reflect on, analyse and communicate the meaning of events, rather than merely passing on what others say about them.

## From adaptation to adaptability

"The network makes assets of ambiguity"
*Stark* (2001:78)

In his research about the digitalisation of information, Pablo Bockzowski (2004) outlines that ambiguity enables actors to move "from adaptation to adaptability" as a guiding operating principle in a volatile economic ecosystem. Studying the ecologies of adaptability, Grabher (2000:6 in Boczkowski, 2004a) writes that the "notion of adaptation implies a retrospective view, reflecting the history of responses to changing environments". Instead, "adaptability looks at the future, indicating the capabilities of coping with unforeseen challenges". Again, we find a Black Swan as defined by Taleb. So, adaptation and adaptability become complementary concepts – kind of the two directions in which Janus's faces are looking at (see Chapter 1) – and the challenge is in the balance between the two, not letting one undermine the other.

The main question is if we start from the assumption that journalism 'has to exist', are traditional outlets coping appropriately with change? Are they ready to encounter adaptability and not just adaptation? And, above all, are they prepared to make sense of this new form of society?

# 6    A culture of innovation embodying the tension between tradition and change

> "Innovations are disruptions to 'equilibrium'"
> *Schumpeter* (1939:XVI)

## In+novo: bringing something new

When the media talks about the journalism crisis, it is commonly associated with the word 'disruption'. I love the simple way Shapiro and Varian define it (1998:ch. 1) as an act of innovation. The etymology of the word 'innovation' describes the act of 'in+*novo*', bringing in something new. In 1963, Mark Blaug (in Barnhurst, 2013:215) wrote that innovation does not consist just in the act of inventing something (the *novus* – 'new'), but it also consists of the "process of absorption" ('bringing') of the invention itself; the act that, according to Kevin Barnhurst, "society and especially businesses undertake to change the circulation of goods and ideas" (2013:215 in Peters and Broersma). Therefore, innovation concerns technological development and social adaptation (then adaptability), involving habits.

Allan (Ch. 10, quoted in Barnhurst, 2013:215) proposes to think of technology innovation as an "interpretative performer" for "journalism cultural transformation" rather than a shaper of what journalists do. This becomes the starting point for rethinking journalism's role. According to Barnhurst, innovation becomes a valuable framework for new narratives such as experimentation, a vital feature of incumbents' strategic responses.

News needs a "path to travel along, and these paths are dependent on technological devices" (Heinrich, 2011:35). Mark Deuze, in his analysis of changes in journalism due to the digital environment, describes technology as a factor influencing journalism from the inside: "[It] must be seen in terms of implementation and how it extends and amplifies previous ways of doing things" (2007:153).

Boczkowski (2004a:ch. 2), an authoritative voice regarding the 'digitalisation of the news' and the evolution of legacy newsrooms through technology, analyses the concept of innovation, and states that the newspapers explored multiple ways to innovate during the first half of the 1990s. Then they narrowed down all their efforts just to personal computer and mobile. There was a shift "from exploring to settling", setting a culture of innovation "marked by a combination of reactive, defensive and pragmatic traits" (48). They have been reactive, waiting for some evident commercial success by being more defensive than offensive, concentrating on understanding effects rather than developing their skills and tools (Ettema, 1989:108, quoted in Boczkowski, 2004), and responding only if short-term returns were evident. In brief, I say, no one adopted an entrepreneurial attitude towards journalism.

To sum up, the news field presents a "culture of innovation [that] embodies the tension between tradition and change", where new horizons are opened but also the status quo is threatened (Boczkowski, 2004:49).

Again, this is why applying entrepreneurship and the entrepreneurial approach, plus the hybrid intrapreneurial mind, is the only way in which news can survive – as we will explore in the next chapters.

### From business to journalism, an interdisciplinary approach

Harvard Business School professor Clayton Christensen, known as 'the master of disruption', studies how changes in technology can impact business performance and strategies. He is quoted in some studies of innovation for journalism (Miller & Reynolds, 2014:92) for his general suggestions about "how to cope with disruption". "Companies must make innovation a high priority and allocate resources (both money and people) to give new ideas a chance to succeed, [...][matching] the technology to the correct market." Innovation requires investments, and the latter are essential decisions that can affect the overall business structure (the news business too).

Moreover, Christensen defines the disruptors' choices as dilemmas: "The dilemmas [are] posed to innovators by the conflicting demands of sustaining and disruptive technologies." In this light, we can say that dilemmas are concerns not just for the disruptor (technology) but also for the disrupted (journalism). They are not just investment choices but also fundamental decisions that can change the functionality and the role of a specific social system: this is the meaning of disruption.

So, what are journalism's dilemmas?

David Skok (2012), from the Nieman Foundation for Journalism at Harvard University, challenges the innovation business study of Christensen and, applying the empiric approach of strategy cases, he formulates (with Christensen himself) "the disruptive innovation in journalism" theory, combining business case studies, innovation theory and journalism business studies.

What arises from this study is that the picture is complicated and understandably pessimistic. Skok's point is that if journalism learns to cope with disruption as other industries did, being aware of the changing ecosystem, the path is more evolutionary than revolutionary. As an institution and a business, this happens because the news has enough means and time to change how it works, cleverly adapting to new technologies. However, the fundamental skilled knowledge of and for 'practising journalism' is the same. News organisations share a value system that can be phrased as "being relevant in people's lives, matter to them and having an impact" (Beckett, 2008:40). To continue to do so, they have to look at the changes as opportunities to seize: the most significant risk for news outlets today is to be left behind by the people they are addressing their service to. Moreover, it is an occasion to let themselves and these people rediscover the unique social function journalism encapsulates.

Disruption has a positive value for me. We live in a disrupted world, so we need to go into it asking, "What would come out of this?" With fear, disruption will never lead you to the positive change it potentially represents.

Tom Goodwin, the author of *Digital Darwinism: Survival of the Fittest in the Age of Business Disruption*, says that the most significant inventions of the last decades did not change anything; they just brought efficiency to our needs. The craziest thing is that they did it without owning anything. Airbnb, which fulfils the need to have a home wherever you go, owns no real estate. Facebook makes us feel closer to our friends, but does not produce content. Uber, the most innovative taxi provider, owns no vehicles.

In the same way, press companies should look at the advent of the network and new technologies to improve their services and expand them.

There, they have more opportunities. However, to innovate, they should first understand that the industrial logic that dominated the mass media ecosystem for decades is gone.

Broersma and Peters (2013), like Anderson, Bell and Shirky (2012), designed a 'Post-Industrial Journalism' theory that tries to cope with the network disruption. The critical point taken into account by this theory is that innovation can internally perform in the journalism field in three changing (and challenged) parts of the news organisation system: the business models, the production process and the paradigms that guide journalism practice and their societal function (Broersma and Peters). Furthermore, five 'core beliefs' are assumed – journalism matters, good journalism has always been subsidised, the Internet wrecks advertising subsidy, and restructuring is, therefore, a forced move. On the other hand, there are many opportunities for doing good work in new ways (Anderson, Bell and Shirky, 2012:37).

The network disruption has been a trauma for journalism, its business model and its practitioners. Therefore, what comes out from these analyses that look at the changes economically, organisationally and culturally, is that the leading players responded to these changes with an industrial logic, a 'logic of yesterday', without understanding that the ecosystem cannot deal with industrial logics any more.

Heinrich (2011:95), recalling Castells and Ince (2003:24), frames this challenge as the moment for news organisations to understand "what kind of node they want to represent according to new tasks and goals": it might be necessary to rethink the "tasks and goals" of these organisations (Broersma and Peters, 2013:7). Their open structure lets news outlets decide "who to connect to, who to dismiss or who to allow" into their network (Heinrich, 2011:95). The degree of openness is the key (strategic) decision that will give a precise image of the news outlet. According to Shapiro and Varian (1998), organisations can choose between two approaches to react to disruption and system challenges: openness towards networks, or closure. Since journalism, when defined, has openness in its ontology (as journalist Charlie Beckett used to repeat in his classes at LSE that I attended), it has to pick openness, which means forging strategic alliances to build meaningful connections in the network economy while continuing to focus on maintaining the consistency of the media institution and brand.

# 7 Technology and journalism: a clash of cultures?

"I do not feel obliged to believe that the same God who has endowed us with sense, reason, and intellect has intended us to forgo their use"
*Galileo Galilei,* Letter to the Grand Duchess Christina

The whole meme of machine versus man is outdated. "Journalism against technology would be akin to being against electricity", Ken Doctor, one of the most renowned news industry analysts and connoisseurs, told me a few years ago during a chat.

I cannot agree more. Technology means tool (*techne*, in Ancient Greek, is the craft, instrument, how a thing is gained) – therefore, technology is morally and ethically neutral; the question is how the technology is deployed. For example, fundamentally, if you use data and analytics to challenge or confirm your assumptions, this is a good thing. However, if you use data and analytics to dictate your content, the technology suddenly makes choices for you, which puts your ethics, mission and value at odds.

Briefly explained, the balance between editorial intuition and judgement and data knowledge and the use of tech tools must be maintained. Even under financial pressure, from the producers' perspective, the data have to inform, not lead, to avoid damaging implications for the content and its quality – and generally the journalistic ethos. Expertise is the actual property of the news organisation, and data cannot replicate it. However, data can move the needle in a 2020s news organisation – publishers can hold a direct relationship with users and offer them the perfect news product: high quality, relevant, informative – on the right platform, at the right time. Only by knowing your user deeply can you do that. This is why "data is the largest catalyst in a news organisation" today, as former FT Chief Data Officer Tom Betts always said.

However, when the iPhone revolution happened (do you remember the Black Swan – the rarity of the event, giant impact and retrospective predictability?), the original sin was committed. There has been a race to conquer the Internet and to use the network at zero costs with no payback. Moreover, social networks enhanced direct relations to the audience and built a strong community. This is a good and bad thing because everyone can talk and potentially reach millions of people without any institutional guarantee. In the world of chaos, as stated, news should be certified and communicated by trustworthy entities and professionals who can guarantee the quality of information plus an analysis supported by knowledge and culture. This should be the basis for every successful news business model.

## The platform battle

Our content has to go where our audiences are, many news publishers think. However, platforms, the main venues where the spread of the content can happen in the network system, are aggregators, distributors, broadcasters and filters. This is why quality publications had and have to deal with them: they are a multifaceted tool.

For instance, the opportunity size of Facebook is incredible, but trying to approach it with the logic of yesterday (as a tool for scalability and profitability to rely on) has dangerous consequences. In fact, in social networks such as Facebook, the visitors browse from one story ('atomised content') to another, without, most of the time, remembering the source, just trusting the stream.

This challenge is an ecosystem matter. Facebook is a garden that grows as long as you stay within it: it tries to give a total experience and so, paradoxically, it needs the web to be closed. One of the beauties of the Internet is the plurality of views and experiences, the same beauty of networked journalism. In this case, the innovation is shutting off the system from that openness. This ecosystem ontology becomes a problem for all the actors involved in the network: readers, users, producers and publishers.

So, legacy organisations should not give out their content to a closed ecosystem freely, just for volume's sake. News outlets would end up being just in charge of creating commodified content: hence, they would become a sort of "brand marketing agency", instead of being a newsroom (to quote Tony Haile). Moreover, publishers have the opportunity to have a first part relationship with their readers through digitalisation. And this is what attracts the platforms to a conversation with news organisations, and this is the competitive news advantage: readers' direct relationship and the uniqueness of the content. Therefore, collaborative partnerships with giants such as Facebook and Google are inevitable. However, news producers have to face the challenge of building a healthy and non-corrupt symbiotic relationship with them, putting their own identity first.

This is also a reader's concern that journalism has to consider when dealing with platforms: looking at the big picture, it is possible to see that this relationship sheds light on some core problems of this network system. In fact, because of its structure, where small groups of self-selected, like-minded people group themselves in hubs and pick individual contents à la carte, social news feeds turn into closed and polarised spaces, reinforcing what the singular user already knows and wants. This system gives more of the same, and this should be the primary concern for each reader, as a citizen: the filter bubble effect.

I was in the UK and doing my Master's at LSE when the Brexit referendum happened. Talking to my British friends in London, they were all quite shocked on 24 June, when the 'leave' result went public. "I would have never expected that: there was nothing like this on my newsfeed!" was the standard response. The Brexit referendum is one of the most prominent and tangible examples of the necessity of journalism in any democratic society. The echo chamber and filter bubble effects have never been as strong as during the months before the referendum date: in part, the lack of plurality and information of about what the vote meant made a difference to the result. The lack of verified information on social media influenced the results, and the overload of fake news changed many people's opinion. The need for a well-informed and quality press has never been proven more strongly than by Brexit.

The COVID-19 pandemic and the surge of an incredible amount of fake news on social media is another example of the need for quality journalism.

It is evident that a filter is required as the sense-making function of journalism for democracy and citizens.

In a nutshell, social media reinforces what you already know by creating a filter bubble. The algorithm gives more of what you already want and you are interested in. Your opinions are backed by your friends (the ones you self-selected) because they share similar views to you. Algorithms provide the same kind of contents tailored to every user, and that is where the echo-chamber ecosystem comes in. Technology forces are not against you, but they are not necessarily made to challenge what you know; they are there to underline what you already knew (whether correct and based on facts or not).

And this is an ethical challenge that poses questions about the background of the actors playing within this space.

Two notable physicists and mathematicians of the past, Newton and Cartesius, were also philosophers and scientists. Their studies came in a historical period when being a scholar and a researcher meant having a holistic culture that included science, theology, philosophy and often literature and classics. The positivist revolution and the need for specialisation after the Industrial Revolution brought a more vertical approach to knowledge and a consequent differentiation of academic and technical studies.

Today we live in a completely different world. In 2021 technology evolution is running so fast that it sounds crazy to waste time studying subjects that fail to pursue a holistic culture.

And yet, in our world, a step back seems necessary. Data, the new gold, show us a picture of the world but they are not enough to represent it per se. A human mind, the human factor able to read them, is required. Lots of professionals involved in media, such as data scientists, social media experts, managers, know this and have learned how to deal with the massive amount of information coming from data and what to do with it. From their daily experience, the need for a more holistic approach to the job can be deduced, an approach driven by solid scientific education, undoubtedly, but with a hint of humanistic knowledge.

The urgency for academic reform emerges, consequently, as a great opportunity to think about new educational paths, where philosophy, anthropology and sociology cross-pollinate with science and numbers to create new professional figures that are able to drive and thrive in the digital era and create disruptive and healthy businesses in the future.

## A matter of ecosystem principles

Once, during a chat over coffee, Michael Skapinker (one of my favourite pens from the FT, now retired) stated that a democratic world without quality, accessible and independent news suffers. This is why it is crucial to study, find and elaborate a way to sustain quality journalism: the price we pay if we don't is a problem for our society as a whole.

It's a fact that today many publishers base their model on social distribution, monetising thanks to reach and volume. To reach the biggest audience possible, many newspapers, caught by the acute anxiety of being the only player not present in the room, chose to be everywhere, losing their brand and values, and spreading their assets among third companies. However, relying on social platforms is dangerous – and not just for ethical reasons. It is a matter of business priorities.

The setting of priorities of a social media producer – optimisation, volumes, advertisements – is quite different from a high-quality 'ideal' publisher. This is not a criticism; I am saying that these two are different jobs with different goals. Acting as a social media manager may be tempting for a publisher, but it is a dangerous role to play. Relying exclusively on social media distribution (when more than 15% of a publisher's traffic is linked to one audience source) means that if the social media company chooses to change their algorithms, and, for instance, de-prioritise news, the publisher will be in great trouble.

However, social media help to find new audiences, experimenting and gaining reach and scale. With over 2.85 billion monthly active users as of the first quarter of 2021, Facebook is the biggest social network worldwide: someone there is a potential reader for a news producer. But there is a defined difference: relying on Facebook or using Facebook. Nevertheless, it should be clear that Facebook has no need for a publisher, has no regard (from a business perspective) for journalism and how it is essential or not for society.

It is pretty obvious that journalism needs Facebook more than Facebook needs journalism.

Google, on the other hand, actually does need journalism. News is a key source for Google's system; people predominantly 'google' about information and news. Google cannot run its business without the content itself, and the Ad Google system wouldn't work (don't forget that more than 80% of Alphabet's revenues come from it – it generated $147 billion in revenue in 2020). The priorities of such an ecosystem are to have good content, available openly and dynamically, within an active networked environment. So Google does need content for its business model. On the other hand, Facebook doesn't. If we all start posting more videos about adorable dogs, lovely holiday shots and excellent succulent food recipes, Facebook will be as happy as if we post more news articles and in-depth analyses about immigration – as long as you stay in, Facebook is happy with any content presented. Facebook does not want you to leave its environment; it is a garden that grows and turns greener (read, makes money) as long as you stay within it; Google grows greener if you jump between platforms, starting from Google, reconnecting it to Google – it blossoms based on the number of roots it can develop.

Google needs the ecosystem to be open; Facebook needs the web to be closed.

So, the fundamental model that drives these two 'technological' entities is different. Publishers need to understand what is aligned with their healthy publisher's business model.

For publishers and their experts (managers, strategists, analysts), it is essential to understand what drives the tech companies to talk to news brands. It is vital to consider that the media ecosystem is no different from any other business. There is an interest behind the conversation and understanding the principles of our interlocutors' business model is fundamental if the partnership is to be fruitful for our journalism.

Journalism should not give everything away to a tech company besides creating content: distribution, users' direct relationships (and data and analytics) and monetisation are critical assets for the news business model. Handing those to a tech partner and losing ownership and control of them, publishers will end up as "a brand marketing agency, formerly known as the newsroom" (to quote Tony Haile again).

### Data – the largest catalyst

One of the key questions I always asked myself when at university was, "Is it possible to define quality quantitatively?"; in other words, what do we mean by quality? Is it possible to measure quality journalism?

Looking at this question not from the product perspective (journalism) but the customer perspective (readers/users), trying to understand and then measure the quality of the customer engagement – rather than the number of customers – can answer the question.

Let's explore how.

As we discussed previously, digitalisation changed news distribution. Publishers who cracked the system were the ones who leveraged this change using data and analytics, and still owned the distribution and direct relationship with customers. They also knew how to measure their performances with appropriate metrics, reflecting business and editorial needs. They were able to share these measures and made them a common language among the organisation so that data was an ally for every department and job.

Being data-informed and data-based when making plans and pitching ideas has always been common practice. However, bringing data into the newsroom has not been the easiest thing.

Former FT chief data officer Tom Betts, whom I had the pleasure to work with on many projects (such as the building and testing of the now well-known consulting firm FT Strategies), always said that "our newsroom needs to be data-informed and not data led".

This is a perfect way to position the role of data. Data help you understand your user (and the 'receiver' of that 'content') and make better decisions on when you write, on which platform and to what length.

On the other hand, there are newsrooms where a data lead has taken over editorial decisions. As discussed before, publications stopped looking at the information value for the sake of volume reach, but looked for the reach only – as THE measure of success. So, in some newsrooms some articles were not approved because they would not 'trend on Twitter' or 'give enough social interactions on Instagram'. This is what killing journalism looks like: guillotining editorial intuition for social media likes. If you start doing this as a publisher, you are on a suicidal mission against your own business. The balance between editorial intuition and machine-data analysis has to be maintained. Otherwise, you should have just machines/AI building your stories, getting algorithms to lead your newsroom rather than humans.

Humans are storytellers – are machines?

I don't mean that machines won't have the capability to be editorially intuitive in the future; but the editorial role will not disappear. The reader experience, serendipity and discovery are crucially needed in order not to create the echo-chamber effect we talked about before. The same happens in the newsroom ecosystem. Suppose you use machine learning and intelligence to tell editorial what can work well with your current and prospective audience. In that case, you might create a self-echo chamber, where you propose to the users more of the same, repeating yourself. Editorial human intelligence and intuition can predict in a more risky but editorially needed way – of course, with the help of technology. To give a high-quality, constructive and informative service to the audiences out there, news organisations need to use editorial experiences as benchmarks and stress tests to make sense of our society. It won't be algorithmically perfect, but it will be the kind of service you expect from journalism.

### Put the user (and data) at the centre of your organisation

Data is certainly not just an editorial matter.

Data is vital for any part of the organisation, as the 2020s news organisation has to put the user at the core of all its business models.

Product, marketing, advertising, business development, events – the user needs to be at the core of everything that news entities plan and bring to the market – a market where everyone is competing for attention. Similarly to the techy social media platforms, the goal should be to create an ecosystem in which users stay and remain the longest, thanks to new languages and new platforms.

We can know everything about our current and prospective customers. Data allows us to do it. But how do you turn the data asset into something actionable for your business?

It is necessary to start smart, bringing actionable insights thanks to data (so that the apparent resistance to data in some departments is defeated). It is then essential to democratise data, make them available to and comprehensible to not data experts. Data is a language: as any language, when spoken by different people, it turns into the common denominator, a common language, to connect organisationally separated departments. A common language also can bring strategy into practice (the execution of the strategy). Thanks to technology, data can be democratised and demystified.

Advanced publishers created 'private' editorial analytics dashboards for the newsroom,[1] empowering journalists with access to rich, real-time

---

[1] Read more about some publishers platforms here: the FT's Lantern https://www.niemanlab.org/2016/03/the-ft-is-launching-a-new-analytics-tool-to-make-metrics-more-understandable-for-its-newsroom/; the *New York Times*'s Stela:

data, helping them better understand the impact of their stories and how different audiences were reacting to them and generally engaging with the news brand's journalism. Listening to users and reading their behaviour and responses through data turns journalism into a better experience in the long run – meaning: a better ecosystem to stay within longer and give attention to – thereby making your news system sustainable.

Being hypothesis-driven, the power of data comes in when tangible results are presented: when they answer key business and editorial questions. Customer data is customer feedback at a scale that makes news organisations successful in digital growth.

Acquisition, retention, understanding the readers and turning them into loyal ones (then members/subscribers): critical questions for the sustainability of a news organisation. Data can clarify and lead you to a data-informed strategic plan.

Again, as I've said before, it is crucial to select the correct data aligned with your strategy. The suggested way is to look at value metrics rather than volume ones. This means publishers should prioritise 'quality reads' ing, the time spent on the platform by one user, over page views or visits lasting seconds. Choosing the right metric can give the news organisation needed long-term sustainability. It is fundamental to learn from the user base and analyse it over time, always being data-informed in the process.

**Advertising metric matters too: from volume to value**

Put users and their data at the centre of your organisation. At the same time, we started with 'how to measure quality and quality journalism'. This means changing not just editorial success metrics but also commercial success ones. So, for example, many publishers adopted CPH, the Cost Per Hour advertising model, a time-based one, a significant innovation in the ads industry.

---

https://www.niemanlab.org/2016/07/the-new-york-times-is-trying-to-narrow-the-distance-between-reporters-and-analytics-data/; The Guardian's Ophan: https://www.journalism.co.uk/news/how-ophan-offers-bespoke-data-to-inform-content-at-the-guardian/s2/a563349/.

Instead of looking at the typical Cost Per Click (CPC) ads model, CPH allows one to understand the quality of the engagement differently – and so the value of it (not its volume!) and, consequently, the value of an advertising campaign (and adjust the pricing accordingly).

This means building a model of journalism that has an engaged, stable, loyal user base – but also an advertising ecosystem that reflects that audience (because it is based on the same quality value metrics). Of

*Figure 5*    Exemplifying the dynamics

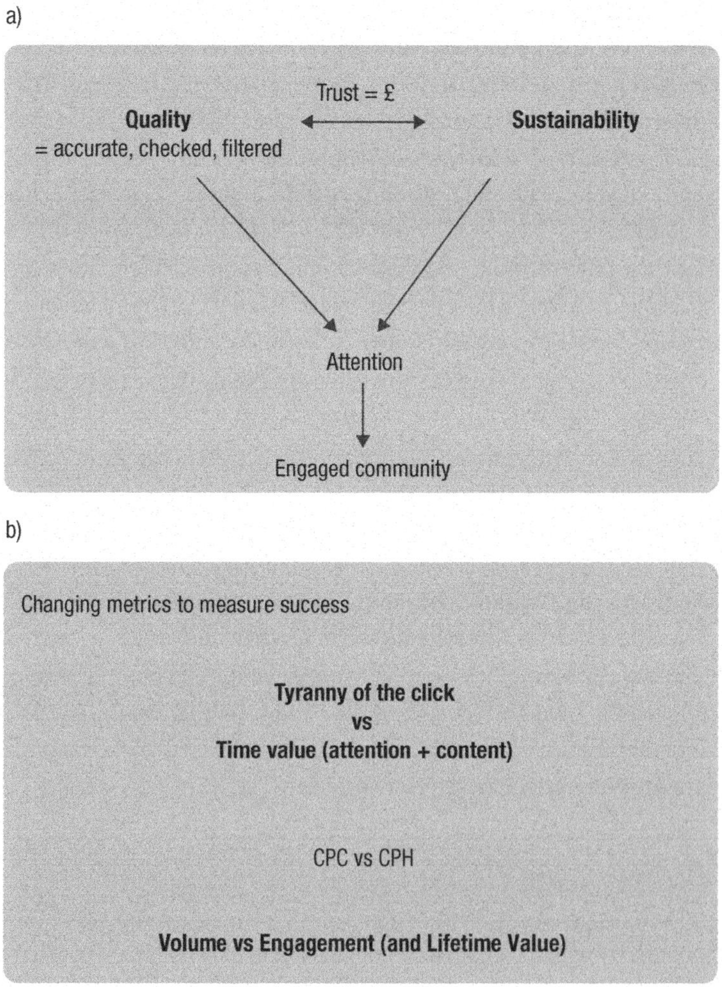

a)

Trust = £

**Quality**    ←——————→    **Sustainability**
= accurate, checked, filtered

Attention

Engaged community

b)

Changing metrics to measure success

**Tyranny of the click**
**vs**
**Time value (attention + content)**

CPC vs CPH

**Volume vs Engagement (and Lifetime Value)**

course, the accurate, checked, filtered content is not data-led (it is data-informed); the data is not leading what to write or not to write. Content is not subject to the tyranny of the click, which has been destroying lots of news organisations in the last decade and killing audience trust . It is based on time value logic, where attention is vital.

We can then simplify the journalism business model so it is based on the monetary value of profit that pays quality attention to the news product. This means the model is based on the value of engagement, instead of the volume of connections. To refer to what I said in Chapter 2, it is all about caring about a smaller number of nodes, cultivating them and having a back and forth constant connection with them. It is not a matter of reaching as many nodes as possible, but a defined number of nodes that have links between each other to be considered an engaged community.

The model is also based on a balance between the two fundamental revenue streams we know are unique to the news space – readers' revenues and advertising revenues.

At the core of the organisation, we should have users. Therefore it is pretty evident that reader revenue is the 'real thing'. Moreover, we know that the advertising business for newspapers is not thriving, and it is subject to the general broad economic context. As discussed in the introduction, the 2020 COVID-19 pandemic killed any ad revenue, and this demonstrates that we cannot rely exclusively on advertising as a source of revenue.

The current keystone for a news organisation is to build a healthy reader revenue-based business model. It can be supported by an advertising system measured with quality metrics that value quality and put the reader's experience first. Users are at the core of news today: only with a reader revenue-based model can we have a long-lasting news organisation, and quality journalism can continue to thrive even in the digital context.

Value over volume should be the common mantra.

# 8　The risk of losing control: the fake news phenomenon

"Lies require commitment"
*Veronica Roth*

In a media world dominated by the chaos previously explained, the risk of losing control, with volume-driven models ruled by numbers and clicks, is enormous. Running after the clicks means forgetting about quality, and forgetting about quality means losing the audience's trust in your organisation. It does not lead you to critical content but sensationalism, and therefore fake news.

This phenomenon is not something new since fake news has always been circulating. The difference is that now it is also profitable and way more difficult to track.

As always, "Historia magistra vitae", history can be an example for reading our contemporary life – as Cicero wrote in *De Oratore*. Continuous repetitions make facts true, even if they are not. "Repeat a lie often enough and it becomes the truth" said Joseph Goebbels, to explain the illusion of truth effect.

Nowadays, we could say "share or retweet a lie enough and it becomes the truth".

Fake news has a very long past. Think about the Christian persecutions, the witch hunts, the Holocaust. All these sociological phenomena and civic crises were solicited by fraudulent information.

A story such as the Dreyfuss Affair remains an exemplary case study for understanding the power of the press and public debate in spreading (fake) news and (mendacious) opinions.[1]

---

[1] At the end of the 19th century, a French officer called Alfred Dreyfuss was condemned and imprisoned for supposedly communicating French military se-

Today, a single tweet by Elon Musk can change the stock fluctuation, and the questions are "Is it true?"; "Should we rely on his tweets?"; "Should we invest in cryptocurrency?". The point here is not the truth, but the reliability. And here is where journalism and its ethically driven business models should take the stage.

And yes, fake news or 'staged news' is definitely profitable. And this is not just in the era of tweet, crypto and the virtual world. It is as old as communications – and, specifically, public relations.

Joseph Goebbels was a German Nazi politician who was the Gauleiter of Berlin, chief propagandist for the Nazi Party and Reich Minister of Propaganda from 1933 to 1945. He was inspired and completely in love with Edward Bernays, universally considered the pioneer of public relations. Bernays was a Jew – fun fact for the Minister of Propaganda for the Third Reich – and Sigmund Freud's nephew. Bernays used Freud's psychoanalytic theory and his belief that unconscious desires drive people as a valuable pivot for shaping his public relations strategies, directing them with a sophisticated business acumen.

When I read his book, *Propaganda*, I was fascinated by it, and I could not believe it had been written and published in 1929 as it seemed so contemporary. This book made me realise how important it is to have reliable journalism and journalists who can hold marketers accountable – because, sometimes, public opinion-shaping can go wrong (see the Goebbels example).

Bernays' influence radically changed the persuasion tactics used by politicians and advertisements up to today. Many of the biggest companies in the 20th-century's market (General Electric, Procter & Gamble, the American Tobacco Company) were his clients. However, the most fantastic anecdote about him is, in my opinion, the bacon and egg story.

Did you know that the so-called energetic American breakfast is one of the biggest pieces of fake news ever? The mind behind it was, indeed, Edward Bernays. In the 1920s the Beech-Nut Packing Company wanted to sell more bacon. Bernays had a solution: he called loads of doctors asking if they agreed that a more nutritious breakfast would be beneficial in terms of energy compared with the traditional lighter one consisting of cereals or a pastry. They said yes. Bernays used this 'scientific' point

crets. It was a political scandal that divided the Third French Republic from 1894 until 1906 when Dreyfuss was finally pardoned and released. It is an example of wrongful conviction and antisemitism, powered by fake news.

to turn the proposed bacon-based meal as the perfect solution to meet doctors' suggestions (even if they never named bacon). The history added the rest: reply to an intentional misstatement often enough, and it becomes the truth. Bacon and eggs is now the iconic American breakfast, with more than 70% of bacon sold to be eaten as the first meal of the day.

It is pretty clear that the main reason behind the spread of fake news is its profitability: it attracts clicks, volumes and attention. This is why fake news is always cleverly built to create sensationalism and astonishment. This attitude is radically changing the language of the press. For example, suppose business models are based on a volume ratio (and emotional responses of the public) rather than a quality content one. In that case, the risk is to attract lots of clicks and interaction but lose the company's credibility – to go after waves of volume to be more profitable. This demonstrates that trust is, indeed, the most valuable asset for a press company – and putting trust at stake is the most dangerous mistake a publisher can make.

To conclude, let me tell you a fun fact. Before the FT, I had a short experience in a London communication agency, freuds Communication, and my hirer was Matthew Freud. Yes, he is the great-grandson of Sigmund and, therefore, related to Edward Bernays. Life, sometimes, is a circle...

---

### HOW TO TURN INTO A FACT-CHECK READER

In a 2019 global survey on social media by Ipsos Public Affairs,[2] 44% of people admitted to having been fooled by fake news at least once.
Consider that outrageous misinformation has an easier time spreading on the web than real news owing to the emotional response all of us, as humans, have when we encounter fake sensational news.
"The SPREAD OF TRUE AND FALSE NEWS ONLINE", an MIT study,[3] found that fictitious stories on Twitter were 70% more likely to get retweeted than real news.

---

[2]    https://www.cigionline.org/sites/default/files/documents/2019%20CIGI-Ipsos%20Global%20Survey%20-%20Part%203%20Social%20Media%2C%20Fake%20News%20%26%20Algorithms.pdf20Part%203%20Social%20Media%2C%20Fake%20News%20%26%20Algorithms.pdf.
[3] https://ide.mit.edu/sites/default/files/publications/2017%20IDE%20Research%20Brief%20False%20News.pdf.

Every time you doubt the reliability of a news piece, here is a quick analysis you can do to verify the accuracy of the information. The goal is to let you learn and master the essential tools of fact-checking to strengthen the critical thinking we should use to evaluate our sources of information.

Take the information piece and start your reading. And follow this step-by-step guide.

### 1. Are you emotionally or rationally reading?

Fake news is such a click and attention success because it is a compelling piece of information. In fact, fraudulent information wants to shock people and stimulate strong instinctive reactions. Moreover, the author of the news addresses the reader directly and establishes a relationship of excessive confidence (suggesting taking actions or making the person reflect on how they feel/how unbearable a situation is, etc.), in which the reader feels personally involved.

To do so, the author uses non-neutral language: the argumentative structure is based on the author's judgement and personal opinions, which are expressed implicitly. In this way, the reader is not informed of a fact (as long as the fact actually occurred), but is given a pre-packaged judgement on the fact itself. This is what manipulation looks like.

This means you must keep your critical thinker brain checking the emotional one (and its natural impulsive responses to such stories).

You can ask yourself some questions: "Why has this news been published? Is it to persuade me or is it neutrally giving me a piece of information? If it is an opinion, is it clear for me as a reader that it is the opinion of an editor? Is the story genuine or is it selling me something? Is it trying to get me to jump to another source that does not seem reliable? Is it asking me to take action after reading?"

### 2. Check the source

Check the web address for the article you are reading or where a post/tweet is directing you. Spelling mistakes or the mimicking of the name of a qualified newspaper or not the usual extensions such as '.com' or '.org' might be suspicious. (e.g. '.infonet'; '.offer').

### 3. Who is the pen behind it?

Review the author's biography and, first of all, discover if he/she even exists. If the author is an actual person, is he/she a credible author of this specific story? Do a bit of digging about the pen behind the news.

### 4. Check data and sources

If an article (or a post, or any piece of news) provides data and figures, the same news should provide the reader with the necessary references to verify the sources and their accuracy.

In many cases, fake news fraudulently uses data and numbers, inventing them from scratch, or decontextualising them, or distorting them for the 'alternative' story they want to tell.

### 5. Evaluate images and videos presented

In the image/Instagram-led society, the news is noticed if it is accompanied by a multimedia piece (e.g. photo or video). Consequently, using a particularly engaging picture is the quickest way to fool readers. As with the use of data, images are often used decontextualised or altered to fit the article topic. Check the source of the image and, if there is none, do not trust it.

### 6. Check linguistic alarms in the text

Fixed narrative schemes are used in any form of storytelling. Think of the oldest myths and fairy tales: there is an anti-hero who creates a break in the initial equilibrium, a victim who is damaged by the anti-hero and a hero who, finally, restores the initial equilibrium by punishing the anti-hero and counterbalances the victim's situation.

Fake news orchestrators use the same schemes to encourage readers to take a stance. The author of the text acts as a 'helper', providing information to the reader and warning them (as a victim).

# 9    Journalism is ontologically r-evolutionary

"The reality is that the elements that make good journalism, and good journalists, will never change. Ignoring the future doesn't mean we can escape it. But paying attention to it means we can shape it"
*Regan* (2000:9)

Through my misfit and intrapreneurial journey, defining what it means to be an intrapreneur and why it is so relevant for news organisations today, I have tried to analyse in a simplified but hopefully holistic way the significant disruptions and challenges that the news ecosystem faces.

In the challenging disruption that the cybernetic network space presents news organisations, we analysed all the 'dilemmas' that news is facing and gave them context: through a definition of the space as chaotic and unpredictable, we have analysed the journalism adaptation to this ecology and its new innovative technologies. Journalism had to face disruption on different levels (e.g. business model, production processes, consumption modalities) and this required resources and investment while juggling traditional values and innovative changes. Moreover, the de-industrialised and de-ritualised concept of 'news' undermined journalism's role within society: the attention scarcity, multiple formats and proliferation of powerful platforms threaten journalism. However, as the Greek etymology of the word 'crisis' teaches, only when a phenomenon is under discussion can we rethink and understand it. Precisely at this critical moment, journalism and its players have the opportunity to analyse how to cope with change and stay true to themselves.

Starting from a more tangible and practical tool as the business model, understanding its changes, we have analysed some responding strategies. The common factor of all of them is experimentation and innovation, thanks to new hybrid roles such as one of news intrapreneurs, polyhedric entrepreneurial minds that bring a different approach – of 'dreamers who do' to the newsroom.

For the 2020s news company strategy, it is fundamental to be trusted and put the audience first. Being audience-driven and data-informed (and not data led) requires new skills such as the data and tech ones. However, editorial knowledge, judgement and intuition are still fundamental and cannot be replicated efficiently by any machine. If technologies are tools to exploit and the platforms (for their seize potential), the sense-making value and inner know-how of the newsroom are irreplaceable. Without quality, accuracy and meaningful content and, therefore, without the audience's trust, journalism would turn just into a mere commodity.

Even if the quality of news is not a measurable concept, it has been indirectly defined here through the different challenges, such as different platforms and tech giants' priorities and the fake news phenomenon. In fact, what has emerged is that the discussion of business cannot absorb the discussion of culture.

It is not the 'what' to disrupt but 'how' to be disruptive. The 'what', the 'culture of journalism', always has to adapt to the ecosystem, otherwise, it could not "make sense of modern life" (Hartley, 2008: 9, 679-691): journalism is ontologically revolutionary per se. In the end, digital disruption and technological innovation (the 'how') become the rediscovering momentum for the core intangible values of journalism as fundamental elements for shaping our chaotic living space and historical circumstances: the sense-making function of journalism has never been so fundamental.

But who works towards the balance between the present and the future of a social entity such as journalism, if not an intrapreneurial mind, with vision, ownership, pragmatism? How to be one and what are the key characteristics of an intrapreneur? How does this relate to the future of news and the younger generation of readers and (news) leaders?

Let's jump to the second part of the book to discover this.

# Part II.
## Intrapreneurship and dreamers who do

# 10    Dreamers who do: *Homo novus*

"Non facit nobilem atrium plenum fumosis imaginibus; nemo in nostram gloriam vixit nec quod ante nos fuit nostrum est: animus facit nobilem, cui ex quācumque condicione supra fortunam licet surgere."

"A hall full of smoke-begrimed busts does not make the nobleman. No past life has been lived to lend us glory, and that which has existed before us is not ours; the soul alone renders us noble, and it may rise superior to Fortune out of any earlier condition, no matter what that condition has been"

*Seneca,* Epistle XLIV (Epistula ad Lucilium XLIV)

Most intrapreneurs and entrepreneurs are modern *homines novi*. In ancient Roman times *homo novus* (literally 'new man') was the Latin expression used to describe the first member of a non-noble family to take political office as consul. Cicero is one of the most famous members of this group: he joined the senatorial elite in Rome with no ancestry or background in politics. At that time, the *homo novus* topos was intended to demonstrate that it did not matter where you were coming from; it mattered where you wanted to go.

Many centuries later, at the beginning of the 19th century, the world became a melting pot of talent following the rise of Napoleon. After the first empire, the crown was in the street, there to be caught, and new generations of young people began to think they could be the next Napoleon, or at least one of the next ministers of France. A new era for the *homo novus* had begun.

Nowadays, learning, studying, connecting and working hard can turn people from the most diverse backgrounds into the contemporary *homines novi*. However, this is definitely not as easy as it sounds, as we will explore in this part of the book by looking at some infrastructural limitations and disruptions, owing to sociological and political set-ups, but there is still, now more than ever, a space for each intrapreneurial mind – especially thanks to corporate projects and policies that can rebalance the initial discrepancies that social and ethnic backgrounds can play when an individual starts a career.

Actually, the hunger of a *homo novus* is quite recognisable and makes an individual competitive and ready to accept the challenges of his career. And, most of all, it becomes a meaningful differentiator especially for women, the *mulieres novae* – to make them leave a mark and, finally, emerge. There is a lot that companies and policies can do to embrace women's entrepreneurial attitude: entrepreneurship is a double chromosome toolkit, as we will explore later in this book.

I never started my career thinking "I am going to be an intrapreneur". That is not quite the dream job formula. I have often been told I was very motivated and full of energy and ideas. I think that my own purpose has always been to bring innovation and to think out of the box, in order to change the status quo where and when nobody else dares to do it. Such a mindset inside an established environment might be seen as revolutionary, but I feel it is more evolutionary, when it comes to updating and adapting an ecosystem to changes brought about by time.

Some of you might ask, what if I don't have the right background? I don't know anything about negotiation, corporate management, budgets – so how can I start a path in such a tricky reality (different from my own)? What matters is to be a driven human. Someone who drives change, drives others, drives the future.

However, when you join a company, do not expect to be a changemaker immediately. One step at a time. Entering the senate thanks to his talents, Cicero took time in climbing the *cursus honorum* – the ladder of office in Rome – to eventually reach the consulship. In my case, it took me 13 months to be able to 'make something happen'.

As I said before, when I joined the FT I used to work as a programme coordinator in a separate start-up owned by the Financial Times Group, the Corporate Learning Alliance (now Headspring), which specialised in executive learning.

My role consisted of being an assistant to a large number of programme and project managers. My daily activities were mainly administrative tasks but being a quick problem-solver was a key advantage for this role – so I trained towards that.

While I was there, I kept looking around. This meant studying the company I had landed at, its ecosystem, its people, its ways of working, its rules and regulations (written and, more importantly, unwritten ones).

While in this role, as I was doing my daily expected tasks, I started using what I call the aerial perspective: looking at things holistically and from above, as if from a hill (you will understand what I mean in a second). My main interest was looking at younger people's perception of the news. How were students introduced to FT content (most of the time this was free, thanks to some deals with universities and schools – check out the FT schools initiatives!),[1] and what were their habits around and relationship with that content? How did I approach the FT and what was my perception of it?

And there I saw a sweet spot for new developments and innovations: everyone knew about the FT but no one thought it was an 'approachable' organisation. An institution, but not a 'place to be' or a resource to talk to. To learn from, for sure, but not to interact with.

However, if there is one thing I noticed about the FT leadership when I started working there, was the open mindedness of everyone around me. People wanted to talk to a student and to know more about my view of journalism – and their journalism. We both had a demand and an offer for quality journalism – but the two never spoke to each other. That is how the FT Talent project was born.

FT Talent was my very first personal project at the FT, the one you would call my 'baby'. It is a programme that attracts younger talent from all over the world, opening the doors of our media group, building a true connection between employers and potential future readers and news leaders. We will explore more deeply what this project entails in this second part of the book.

You might ask: how to start a changemaking project when you are just joining a company and you are considered a junior talent?

The answer is in the intrapreneurial approach to this journey in the media world.

As already mentioned, I was first an observer, a systematic one, and I picked my niche: the future of quality news and how to attract younger people to the traditional world.

---

[1] Free for Schools project by FT: see https://www.ft.com/content/7ab6a9ec-1c4c-11e8-aaca-4574d7dabfb6.

# 11 The aerial view and the mastering of contamination

"To develop a complete mind: Study the science of art; Study the art of science. Learn how to see. Realize that everything connects to everything else"
*Leonardo da Vinci*

Here is where the concept of 'aerial view' came to my mind years after I first experienced it. I have always dreamt about flying. Not for the sensation of being surrounded by the air (a motorbike is enough for that, thanks!), but for seeing things from above, from a wider standpoint. Embracing a horizontal view of facts, and trying to discover what ties things together is something I have always found fascinating. The first time that I flew I was obsessively wondering how amazing it would be to see Bologna from above; if the shape that we see on the maps is the real one. Which colours match the grass, what kind of magic do we miss from below? Someone else asked himself these questions (and someone for sure I'm not comparing myself to!): Leonardo da Vinci. We can definitely consider him an entrepreneur, with a brilliant entrepreneurial mind, indeed, for his approach to knowledge and curiosity. He was the first one to theorise the 'aerial' – or colour – perspective, and thanks to that, he was able to start painting with true realism. His theories come from an accurate observation of nature and its phenomena. In his theories, the linear perspective comes first, to understand the true geometry of things, but then an aerial perspective (observation of lights and shadows) should be investigated in order to realistically represent the world on the canvas or the paper. Similarly, an intrapreneur should be able to picture his/her industry, or company, with a holistic view, with the goal of innovating while keeping in mind the true representation of the space he/she is playing within.

Being an intrapreneur means becoming a master of connections: linking separate parts, needs, wants. It involves a skillset that should be taught in schools much more widely than it is today. That's why I loved studying ancient languages such as Ancient Greek and Roman Latin so much: to translate you need to be able to connect different words and meanings, but also you need to appreciate the overall sense of the piece you are translating. The meaning influences your choice of words for the translation. This, Leonardo's aerial perspective, is key for innovators.

Perspective and joining the dots, connecting and allowing to be contaminated by other ideas and fields, we say. This is the formula for innovation and entrepreneurship.

When I think about intrapreneurial minds, I always think about Giuseppe Garibaldi. When he first arrived in New York with Bovi Campeggi, a patriot from Bologna, on 30 July 1850, the 'red republicans' – Italians and also French, Hungarians, Polish, Germans – received him as a hero. He moved to Staten Island, to a small country house called Clifton, with other Italians. Among them was Antonio Meucci.

To afford their life in New York, this miscellaneous group started to produce salami and sausages. A funny story tells that once, while cutting the raw meat, Bovi Campeggi had an injury, and part of his finger ended up in the mixture. He laughed. "No worries, it's all meat. We will eat republican salami!"

Maybe because of this not overly professional attitude, the business did not have the expected success and the team abandoned it soon. As we all know, necessity is the mother of invention, so the group converted the space for food production into a candle factory. Imagine what could happen when the status quo challenger, the hero of the two worlds, Garibaldi, worked closely with the one who had changed the world for good with his invention of the first telephone, Meucci. During that experience Garibaldi learnt about methodology, but also about energy. Meucci learnt about leadership. Contamination is, again, the key for innovation.

This story tells us that the urge for funds and money is the main source for innovative and entrepreneurial thinking. This is an urge media companies feel every day: the need to be relevant and economically sustainable.

We all know of Royal Dutch Shell, the British/Dutch multinational oil and gas company, worth US$180.5 billion (2020) and with 86,000 employees (2021). Would you expect to find in its largest division (Exploration and Production) an entrepreneurial urge? Probably not. And yet by late 1996 its director of research and technical services, Tim Warren, and his team had realised that without a radical innovation they were unlikely to meet their earning targets. They started to feel the pressure for new business models. Tim Warren was clear that his employees were the key for the disruption, and an uncountable resource for fresh and nonlinear ideas. He gave them $20 million to sustain game-changing ideas and projects, calling it the GameChanger Process. It was November 1996. Within the Innovation Lab, a three-day event designed by consultants from Strategos, the employees were encouraged to think out of the box, and explore innovation strategies from other businesses. By the end of the event, 240 new ideas had been designed by a new kind of professional: the internal entrepreneur, the intrapreneur. The Innovation Lab was followed by the Action Lab, where credible venture plans were designed, and by 100-day Action Plans, consisting of low-risk ways of putting the ideas into practice. In early 1999, not only were four of the company's largest initiatives born within the GameChanger Process, but Shell had also found that entrepreneurial zeal was the key for a radical, innovative push within its giant structure.

In the 2020s the programme is still active: Shell has interacted with more than 5,000 innovators around the globe, helping them turn more than 150 ideas into reality.

What are the media doing to be entrepreneurial, innovative, ever evolving? Is it possible in this industry and how can resistance to change be faced?

# 12    Challenge the system

"Aut inveniam viam aut faciam.
I shall either find a way or make one"
*Latin proverb attributed to Hannibal, the response when he was told it was impossible to cross the Alps by elephant*

When I joined the FT I was told "We need to work with respectful audacity."

I found this a very interesting way to put it: short, effective, like an ad. It gave a sense of the balance structure to maintain and suggested the right way to put innovation to work. It turned out to be my mantra for working within the news industry.

In terms of terminology, I like to use 'guerrilla gardening' to define the right to explore, test, examine, study, fail – for employees – and to be entrepreneurial. Guerrilla gardening is a spontaneous movement that appeared in the 1970s in the New York area. It is the act of gardening on land that the gardeners do not have the legal right to cultivate, such as abandoned sites, areas that are not being cared for.

I like to think of intrapreneurship as an endogenous guerrilla gardening movement – it means an internal rebellion, quality led, to improve things in small mission groups. In fact, we can consider intrapreneurs as diplomatic rebels, balancing the status quo challenger spirit with diplomatic tactics.

When I first pitched FT Talent I needed to act like a politician, as does everyone in a managerial, creative, innovative, disruptive role. It doesn't matter about the hierarchy; what matters is the idea: if the idea is going to change the cards on the table, well, you will face resistance. Resistance to change, which we explored in the first part of the book, is typical of the news industry: this is why I believe that talking about entrepreneurship in this ecosystem and trying to take a few lessons from it can be beneficial for many innovators out there.

The antidote to resistance is perseverance (basically, stubbornness with a purpose).

Resistance to change comes from three traps (Ahuka and Lampoert, 2001):

1. familiarity trap: favouring the familiar/known over the unfamiliar/unknown (risker);
2. maturity trap: going for the mature over the nascent;
3. propinquity trap: favouring proximity to existing solutions rather than new solutions.

An intrapreneur focuses all his/her energy not on fighting the old but on building the new. Most of the time, intrapreneurs start at a very early stage in their career lives: creativity flies higher at a younger age when some world realities and facts have not corrupted the soul. As Picasso said, "Every child is an artist. The problem is staying an artist when you grow up." Intrapreneurs are creative thinkers, a quality that is an advantage when everything you have to focus on is the new, respecting the old. But it can, of course, create some barriers. Most of the time, organisational culture does not support radical innovations and changes owing to its hierarchies and rigid structures. Most of the time, big companies have two approaches to innovation, which often end up in incremental improvements and optimisations rather than disruptive innovations:

1. R&D departments – big companies create a separate space (they often call it a 'lab') with a small number of people to develop new products. Owing to the different context they act in and the limited interactivity with the bigger picture and structural underinvestment in these departments, their impact is minor. Therefore, these structures end up just optimising what has already been created (like improving an existing product).
2. emulating VC (Venture Capitalist) dynamics: companies build accelerators and incubators to get access to an outsider perspective on change (Deloitte, 2015) – where early-stage start-ups (a bit like consultants, often involved in the innovation game) come in and advise about radical innovations the company always knew

about but never dared to implement. The outsider perspective is quite often forgotten when the corporation goes back to business as usual.

Neither of these two approaches is the one of the intrapreneurial paradigm. The intrapreneur relies not on a department and his/her expected role, but thinks with a bottom-up approach, relating to individual employees taking and believing in an initiative to improve their company as a whole. There is a strong sense of belonging within the intrapreneur community: they strongly feel connected with the culture and the mission of their company, and they feel as if by operating within a 'guerrilla garden space' they can achieve more for the sake of the future of their organisation. They foster disruption with entrepreneurial behaviour: knowing the organisational structures but acting at its boundaries, diversifying processes and developing new capabilities, most of the time being contaminated by other industries' inspirations, they challenge the status quo, putting people and their ideas at the core of change.

Thanks to the guerrilla garden space, where small groups of people have the time to cultivate their ideas, many great new experiments can turn a company into a more valuable and innovative – and, above all, ready-for-change players in the industry.

When Steve Jobs and 20 Apple employees separately developed the Apple Macintosh computer, they worked on the side, freely, often neglecting structures and rules of the organisation – for the sake of their vision. The radical product and service innovations this team was able to deliver was something R&D had failed to generate before, demonstrating that acting within guerrilla intrapreneurial dynamics could pay off in terms of company growth and competitive advantage. The group was committed to achieving success and it turned out to be an infectious attitude: more people within the larger company started pushing for increasing innovations, changing the culture.

# 13    Empathy and adaptability: be a great listener

"We have two ears and one mouth, so we should listen more than we say"
*Zeno of Citium, as quoted by Diogenes Laërtius*

## The art of listening

There is a difference between politeness and education.

The former is part of your education as a human being in a society (politeness from the Latin *politus*, meaning 'refined, elegant, accomplished'; the meaning 'behaving courteously, showing consideration for others' is by 1748 implied in the word 'politely'), while the latter is a form of institutionalised education (the education since mid-16th century English, from Latin *educatio*, from the verb *educare* – 'to lead out').

An educated person is a knower of things. A polite person is so because of a relationship with a group – a community. He/she is open to the world, and is the one who is able to intercept the non-linearity of things. This is what intrapreneurs do: they look for spots, inconsistencies, the imperfection of things: basically, their humanity.

As Brunello Cucinelli, an enlightened and mystic entrepreneur, said, "a change maker is a human that aspires to go, not in an arrogant way, for a lifelong revolution". A 'Dreamer Who Does' can intercept emotions in things and people.

"Tears are the gasoline of the soul", someone said. And I'd add that tears are the gasoline of a successful business too. Emotions, vulnerability and active listening are essential for a great dreamer and doer. This is why empathy is critical, like many other soft skills.

You need to understand better who is in front of you – a boss, a top executive, a client, a colleague – and adapt your manner and style to the one you are approaching. When you pitch your idea (and, before this, involve someone else in your innovation process), this is a fundamental skill. Consequently, adaptability follows empathy – another unique tool for an innovator.

Being empathetic is, in fact, critical to being a good leader.

Leaders who lacked empathy struggled in 2020.

In December 2020, Deloitte reported that 61% of 3,600 executives surveyed in 96 countries were focused on transforming the workplace, double pre-pandemic levels. Specifically, leaders were shifting away from priorities such as optimising automation toward building a workplace around the strengths of human resources.

I think it is fair (if paid, of course!) to be assigned to such roles: you can come from the best universities, but we all know that the corporate world is another thing. It means you need to start from somewhere that gives you some grounding and space for you to listen and understand the company you are part of. I believe that we have been given a general misconception about internships, graduate schemes and junior roles in fields that we have not studied for. This is a matter of frustration for many students and younger talents I had the chance to talk to. However, I believe a great change of perspective is needed.

While I was a coordinator, it was my job to not feel submerged by my daily tasks but allow myself to look around. This meant studying the company I landed at, its ecosystem, its people, its ways of working, its rules and regulations (written and, more importantly, unwritten ones). However, I was conscious and still am that I cannot undertake all the innovations myself. I had and have a specific job to do, with certain duties and responsibilities. When you start your career in a big company, make sure you do an excellent job at what you are expected to do by your job description. That is your priority. Your entrepreneurial spirit comes out when you can challenge yourself and that same job description, maybe posing a business question to something you are doing – but it's your skill to find time to do so. But again, as said, being an intrapreneur is not a 9am to 6pm role.

So finding time (a branch of time management) should be something to prioritise in the way you approach your work.

This has always been my strategy: empathy and active listening to the people around me and the problems/questions they were trying to solve.

Plutarch wrote that he solved 50% of his problems by just listening to others. In his pamphlet "The art of listening" (Περὶ τοῦ ἀκούειν – De recta ratione audiendi) he warns against the desire to express one's opinion before being ready to do so: "How many do we see making mistakes, practising speaking before having acquired the habit of listening?" Plutarch wrote referring to young people. I might look contradictory here. What I am trying to say is that no experience is a waste. Ever. What matters is your approach to it – and your humble approach to a career sprint. You should have an incremental approach to your career: pick things up, learn and upskill yourself gradually. Success does not happen overnight. Every step is worthy: your satisfaction is based on hard work, consistency, hunger and focus.

Being curious and an active listener is vital when you join a corporate space and you want to innovate. You cannot innovate if you are not entirely aware of the area you are playing within – and the people there. You need to have a think-action approach, fighting to implement your vision when you have the chance to. But as said before, being a visionary thinker means investing much time in your research and a deep understanding of the place you are working in. Start from an organisational chart.

Being at entry level is not a curse. Being able to see all the wants and needs for a successful project, being aware of 'behind the scenes' areas will make you a well-rounded professional and a much better leader. Having been in admin, managing all your bosses' presentations and event catering, the AV set up and then the clients' needs – well, this will allow you to budget and estimate deliveries and results for any project you will be managing. But, above all, it will make you way more of an empathic professional to work with. You have been there, you know how it feels, and you can relate so much more to your colleagues – and their tasks.

### Feeling a caretaker, not an owner: give back and build Vitruvian architectures

"The only thing worse than being blind is having sight and no vision"
*Helen Keller*

How can you have an entrepreneurial view of things – meaning a long-term vision for your project?

Management requires quick wins and sometimes a very short-term view of plans. As a first step every time you approach a new question I'd encourage you to think about three stages of resolutions and effects: how will they play out in a year, in five years, in ten years.

Working on a ten-year span in the media/news industry might be slightly unhelpful. As we saw in the first part of the book, in just ten years the industry completely changed owing to new technologies (primarily the iPhone). However, the sociological and, generally, macroeconomics effects of any projects are always a long-term change, so it is worth putting them on your plan when you are organising your thoughts – and, above all, when you are preparing your pitch.

Genius, inspiration and creativity also require concreteness and pragmatism. Taking risks, not having a sense of fear, or, even worse, submission. Thinking about hope in your projects. The new cultural revolution is all about that.

I think the winning attitude should be the one of a caretaker, not an owner. Vitruvio used to say that architecture should pursue beauty, usefulness and solidity ("Firmitas, utilitas, venustas" – in *De Architectura*). His idea was to build something that could last, something we then take care of. This is the entrepreneurial spirit. Do not do something for ourselves, but for a long-lasting project to leave a legacy. This is, maybe, another way to read blue-sky thinking. Not only be a dreamer but be a carer, someone who can protect and hand down a vision. Everyone can be an entrepreneur if you think about it.

When I was a student, a senior leader opened the door of the *Financial Times* and gave a chance to a girl with a dream. Now that the girl has turned into a woman with a career, she has the objective of giving her a chance back. That is why I believe so profoundly in the FT Talent challenge because it creates a dream, and with the dream comes the vision of a more open and inclusive work environment. I am convinced that any student in the world should have the same opportunity that I had and, once having entered the corporate game, should do the same for others. Give the others what you had the chance to receive, and most of all, do it immediately, without waiting to be a senior manager. Everyone, even an intern, has a strong impact on this process. This is a mentality that is increasing and is shared within my generation. This is the key concept of giving back, being a carer, the purpose of my entire career path.

# 14　Why should media organisations push for intrapreneurship?

"If you hire people just because they can do a job, they'll work for your money. But if you hire people who believe what you believe, they'll work for you with blood and sweat and tears"
*Simon Sinek*

## Breeding intrapreneurs

Companies are competing for the best talents out there. So sophisticated admission processes, mostly AI-led, try to find the best-fitting profiles.

What I have noticed in the field is the short-term vision in most of the HR process.

This involves looking at new employees as needed to fit a particular role, with a very determined job description and skill set. If this is good in terms of efficiency, it usually excludes diverse ways of thinking and backgrounds as much as creative thinkers. Intrapreneurs do not fit a single profile but are instead an eclectic mix of skills, summed up in entrepreneurial and go-getter personalities. First of all, they have an intrinsic motivation to change the status quo (of a rule, process, product, old way of doing things) and are willing to create new systems and processes. They are also aware that they should create value that has a social and environmental impact. They inspire change and they are meaningful disruption seekers. And, last but not least, they should help attract and retain employees, even if they are not the hirers.

However, when talent acquisition is established, it tends to think in a very highly managerial way rather than entrepreneurial, meaning it goes for the short-term solution, forgetting the longer view on a talent acquired. In contrast, they should be aware that they are leading their company into the future. Therefore, a long-term vision is compulsory.

This goes along with the silo logic typical of larger and established companies.

However, let's look at the way emerging tech groups organise their talent acquisition. We could learn something interesting here: talent is intertwined with M&A strategies, meaning that acquiring a new company means acquiring a specific product/process but it is, most of the time, acquiring an uncovered talent. So the way Silicon Valley looks at critical venture development, it's about the talent strategy: what capabilities and people are they getting out of that acquisition?

Silicon Valley is based not on resource allocation but resource attraction – a fundamental distinction. If an idea is valuable, it will attract both money and talent immediately.

Silicon Valley CEOs know that if their people don't sense a compelling vision and significant upside, they will leave.

Disney is another example of virtue in this sense. It is indeed one of the companies that better understood the importance of moving its best talents to non-traditional business areas (theatre production, hotels, live-animal theme parks), giving them a sense of belonging, a parochialistic faith in the company, grown from the chance to work on something unique and new.

Employees should be aware that the best way to thrive and win is by being part of something that never existed before. This internal attitude encourages bravery in taking risks and investing in something out of the ordinary. It means incentivising those who abandon the secure for the untested. It means, in two words, cultivating entrepreneurs, and investing in the future by standing on the most intrepid souls' shoulders.

### How to spot an intrepid soul: common DNA traits

When it comes to intrapreneurs, it is not just about finding them externally (hiring or through M&A) but being able to recognise them internally.

HR and the management can trace them, as intrapreneurs, even if they do not fit a single profile, because they follow similar patterns in their career approach.

1. *Intrapreneurs look for 'sweet spots' within the company*: scouting opportunities or markets to solve an already existing problem, collecting in-

sights and information, comparing them to industry and market trends and making a case. From vision to planning to complete implementation, they look for new ideas that they can realise and build from scratch. And nobody asked them to do this – and, most of the time, it's not expected from them (basically, it's not written down in their job description when they sign their employment contract).

The above turns out to be a critical competitive advantage for them as employees as they exceed expectations, but also for the company: high performers are the ones that take organisations to the next level.

2. *Intrapreneurs are visionary thinkers*: bringing a 360-degree overview of each project and always bringing their thinking back to the complete picture. Having an idea is different from having a vision. When we think about intrapreneurs or innovators in general, we have this misconception that they are generalists and blue-sky thinkers. This is wrong. There are many ideas out there – and executives of large companies are constantly exposed to them. However, visionaries can build upon the ideation process and transform it into one actionable plan that goes in one precise direction, the vision. Neophyte idea generation is about conceiving of a variety of things quickly; vision generation is about the "relentless exploration" and research of one deep and robust new way of seeing the world (Verganti, 2010).[1] It goes in one direction only.

However, visionary thinkers need to clearly understand the ecosystem they are acting with – so a horizontal/aerial perspective on the surroundings (Leonardo's!). What is the company standing for? What are the overarching value statements it is delivering? This inside-out position makes them closer to the external targets (specific user bases, customer groups, etc.) and also, as their perspective is the one of the 'outsider', they need to motivate others to engage with their vision, bring them on board – and believe in it. Vision building is about convergence. This is why they are great leaders and motivators – but also efficient managers and excellent project managers. In fact, they have to be responsible for delegating tasks and managing a project ('managers') successfully, but also they need to bring out the best in people, inspire them and work towards a common and shared goal ('leaders').

---

[1] You can find the article at: https://hbr.org/2010/03/having-ideas-versus-having-a-vision.

Dealing with resistance, they have limited access to resources, and they need to work outside the 9–5 schedule, so they do not over-engineer their ideas; intrapreneurs focus on the core (e.g. delivering an efficient MVP [minimum viable product], data lead), engaging a limited and unique group of people. It means they understand the current workforce they belong to and whom to involve (and how much). It means that they are great observers of the social ecosystem that is a company. It means that they can grow the bottom line with the support of the top one (senior management): they motivate and involve others, who learn something different and work on something new (most of the time this is a bit more exciting than their current daily tasks), but they can do so only if they have internal champions who believe in them. The networking skills intrapreneurs have are valuable: internal and external (this leads to meaningful partnerships with other companies or PR actions – people get to know the intrapreneur's vision, so his/her company idea progresses more quickly than 'ordinary' new products/processes). Ideas are neutral, but thoughts are culturally biased visions: to be complete, they need to design a new 'world', disrupting existing paradigms and building new frameworks (Verganti, 2010).

3. *Intrapreneurs want rapidity for their vision.* They do not have time for hierarchies, processes, over-complications. They have to show their idea makes sense, which means they want to test it. And test it quickly. The speed with which the market is served is critical when you find a sweet spot in it. There are incredible minds out there who are probably already thinking about a solution to a particular problem. Intrapreneurs know this well, so they want to cut time-to-market deadlines, being proactive, bold and flexible risk-takers. Moreover, their go-getter mindset is an actual cost saving for larger companies and a tremendous competitive advantage: speedy problem-solvers and innovators kill useless development cycles.

4. *Intrapreneurs have some key characteristics* (we can all learn and develop – you don't need to be born with them!). They are trustworthy, meaning that they are perceived as reliable professionals. They commit to do what they said they will deliver, so you can rely on them practising what they are preaching. Their key characteristic is being open-minded and curious. They know what they want to achieve and where they want to go,

but they still listen to other people's opinions and options to turn their role into a multifaceted one, always hybrid and evolving. To do so, they need to be perceptive of any meaningful stimuli: they have their eyes open, always eager to learn from other experiences and integrate them into their journey. They are 'dreamers who do': the doer part comes out as time-bound, time effective and solution-driven. They know how not to waste their time – as they understand how precious it is – and they see life as a path full of problems. Therefore they know that to be a 'useful mind' they need to bring a solution (or at least frame themselves as problem-solvers)

Intrapreneurs need to be motivated within the large structure they act in, not just through financial rewards (often attached to their projects and successes), but also through non-financial means, intangible rewards such as peer recognition, awards, the chance to talk to the board or CEO, opportunities for public speaking as a company ambassador, an international move to another country and so on. These are pretty life-changing opportunities that money cannot buy.

It might be surprising to many of you, especially younger readers, but as the research "The relationship between pay and job satisfaction: A Meta-Analysis of the Literature" by Judge, Piccolo and colleagues (2010) shows, "the notion that high pay leads to high levels of satisfaction is not without debate". Despite the common thinking, results of the paper suggest that "pay level is only marginally related to satisfaction". (Cumulating across 115 correlations from 92 independent samples, the pay level was correlated .15 with job satisfaction and .23 with pay satisfaction.)

These results have obvious implications for people management: if we want a committed, happy and satisfied workforce, money is not the answer. Money does not buy engagement. Recognition, intangible rewards, life-changing opportunities do.

# 15 Adriano Olivetti: the dreamer who inspired Steve Jobs

## Adriano Olivetti: the Italian dreamer who did

> "Often the term utopia is the most convenient way to liquidate what one does not have the desire, capacity or courage to do. A dream feels like a dream until you start working on it. And then it can become something infinitely greater"
> *Adriano Olivetti*

Experimentation is key to any industry and in any emerging or established companies.

People need to be allowed to innovate instead of being ordered to do so.

This includes experimenting and subsequently failing, but freely and early – so that learning can outweigh the effort of starting from scratch.

Steve Jobs understood the importance of freedom and creative thinking – and the importance of 'breeding intrapreneurs' – but we can confidently say he was inspired to do so by an Italian mind – Adriano Olivetti.

You may have heard of Olivetti (1901–1960), the Italian computer pioneer and typewriter guru from Ivrea, in the north of Italy: an entrepreneur who could inspire others to bring an innovative attitude to work, being 'dreamers who do'. Intrapreneurs blossom within a modern corporate context; corporations, as any spin-off of our human society, are complicated entities. As companies are made of men and women, no doubt working well with joy stimulates and produces innovation – what intrapreneurs need as air to do their job correctly.

Olivetti was the kind of factory owner who used to push for entrepreneurship in his colleagues from any level of the company hierarchy: the protagonists in the company's history were not only the top management.

Workers were encouraged to express their proactive and curious initiatives freely, knowing that the company was open to contamination: humanistic and technical-engineering cultures were mixed and matched to create a healthy and exciting working environment. Moreover, personal capabilities rather than seats in the hierarchy made people move up the company ladder: factory workers became general managers, intellectuals and people from a Humanities background (the 'humanists') held decision-maker roles, technicians collaborated with economists and designers – all working together, believing that contamination is vital for innovation.

Olivetti transformed the typewriter factory from a simple workplace into a social and sharing reality. He strongly believed in the sense of community and happiness, and he tried to shape the best society possible for his workers. Innovation was a multifaceted concept for Olivetti: from technical improvement to design integrations, he also interpreted it as a search for the beauty of forms. This quest meant an exceptional commitment to product design but, more than anything, beauty for everything surrounding the factory and its people: warehouses, laboratories, offices, shops. Any workplace was built on a beautiful human scale, because Olivetti understood that the ecosystem of those who work in a company should be full of positive stimuli.

In fact, he was convinced that "happiness generates efficiency", and therefore he used to pay his workers higher salaries than his competitors. In addition, he provided vocational education, social services, cultural activities, transport and environmentally friendly nurseries, schools and houses around his industry for all his co-workers.

"The factory cannot look at the index of the profit," he used to say. "It must distribute wealth, culture, services, and democracy. I think about the factory for men, not the men for the factory."

In the same way, the intrapreneurial mind we have been describing in this second part of the book should refer to human capital and start from there, to build a healthier business in a healthier environment.

Olivetti was an entrepreneur with a remarkable intuition towards innovation: he was actively aware of international markets and overseas ideas and a far-sighted selector of his collaborators: as I've said, innovation is a matter of people.

Olivetti was capable of looking at things with an 'aerial view', and he could select partners based on their capabilities and, above all, their human factors and perspectives on the future of the company (more as a social entity than 'just' a business). His goal was to put together small teams of enthusiastic, heterodox and innovative talents to create beautiful innovations that could change – and simplify – people's lives.

Moreover, he often chose young people, allowing them to grow no matter their backgrounds: Olivetti realised that he needed younger forces to bring innovation to the next level for his company and his technical innovations. Examples were the Italian-Chinese Mario Tchou, whom he recruited at Columbia University in New York, and the young engineer Pier Giorgio Perotto, who came from Fiat.[1] Both of them were able to be leaders of small teams and experimental labs – they were able to be intrapreneurs. And it turned out that their projects were some of the most glorious products ever designed by the Olivetti factory.

In the late 1950s, Olivetti produced the ELEA 9003 and Program 101,[2] the first electronic processor in Europe and the first desktop computer in the world.[3] Both of these products were designed by the two young minds who had been recruited personally by Olivetti: Mario Tchou, who was 35 years old, and Pier Giorgio Perotto, who was 27 years old.

As with every dreamy tale, this one ended pretty tragically. In a moment of solid success (Olivetti was present on all major international markets, it had just acquired Underwood, the leading US typewriter manufacturer, and had approximately 36,000 employees), Adriano Olivetti suddenly died on 27 February 1960, during a train journey from Milan to Lausanne.

He made an unforgettable impact on Italian and European industry, which made us dream of an Italian Silicon Valley.

This dream was still of great importance and inspiration for one of the Silicon Valley gurus, Steve Jobs.

----

[1] Fiat Automobiles SpA is an Italian automobile manufacturer. In the 1950s it was one of the most prominent Italian companies.

[2] ELEA stands for Elaboratore Elettronico Aritmetico (Arithmetical Electronic Computer, which was changed to Elaboratore Elettronico Automatico for marketing reasons) and was chosen with reference to the ancient Greek colony of Elea, home of the Eleatic school of philosophy. Why this philosophy? It took logical standards of clarity and necessity to be the criteria of truth – quite appropriate for the first solid-state computer designed and manufactured in Italy.

[3] NASA purchased the P101 to study and calculate the phases of the elliptical orbits that allowed the Apollo 11 moon landing in 1969.

### Adriano Olivetti and Steve Jobs: aesthetic elective affinities

It is possible to explore the aesthetic continuity of global consumer icons, even when it comes to one of the most disruptive industries, such as technology.

Comparing the story of Adriano Olivetti, the typewriter master from Italy, and the genius of Steve Jobs, we can discover the importance of architecture and design for Apple. This company turned beauty into a strategic asset and competitive advantage, as Olivetti had 60 years before.

Indeed, Apple turns out to have partly inherited, impressively and surprisingly, the Olivetti minimalism disruptive model, specifically in showroom design.

Olivetti and Jobs were both polyhedric and innovative entrepreneurs, but few know the considerable influence that the Italian almost utopian man had on Jobs' strategies and products. One tangible example is the importance of calligraphy to both of them: during job interviews Olivetti used to give a calligraphy test to all the candidates, while Jobs attended a calligraphy course at Portland's Reed College and considered it pivotal in his life. Moreover, architects played an essential role in both companies: hugely influential in the design of the showroom, Jobs was obsessed with Olivetti's artefacts and stores, from the shape and the colours to the materials. In fact, when it came to designing the first Apple store in 2001, Walter Isaacson, Jobs' biographer, writes that Jobs hired Florentine designers to inspect the cutting and layout of the tiles to use in the store: he wanted it to be covered with these stones directly shipped from Florence, the same grey-blue sandstone he had seen in 1985, during an Italian trip, on the sidewalks. The same material choice had been used for the Olivetti floors 50 years before (see Figure 6).

More unexpectedly, a 26-year-old Jobs "come(s) to revere the Italian designers, and it was an amazing inspiration": he took part in the International Design Conference in Aspen in 1983, and there he met the Italian "Great Beauty" pillars – the filmmaker Bernardo Bertolucci (*Last Tango in Paris*, *The Dreamers*), the automobile designer Sergio Pininfarina (Ferrari, Maserati, Cadillac, Bentley, to name a few), the Fiat heiress Susanna Agnelli and, above all, the Olivetti designer Mario Bellini. Bellini was the one who galvanised Jobs' approach to product perfection: with his speech describing product design centricity in the Olivetti mindset and the imperative role of beauty, Bellini impressed Jobs

*Figure 6*    Olivetti stores in New York and St Gallen, Switzerland

Photo by Erich Hartmann/Magnum Photos

*Source*: futurimagazine.it

so much that the Californian personally visited and repeatedly called the Italian artist, offering him the chance to design new products for Apple. Bellini refused this opportunity but still influenced Jobs mindset, as did the whole Olivetti company: essential figures when shaping the 'Apple concept' were Carlo Scarpa and Ettore Sottsass, both key Olivetti players and the main creators of Olivetti showrooms around the world. The minimal and elegant aesthetics of the Apple design, from stores to products, are visual proof of the Italian beauty and taste heritage that the Californian brand is still, silently, infused with.

# 16  People buying it: yourself and the idea

## How to assure disruptive innovation success

"Big breakthrough ideas often seem nuts the first time you see them"
*Marc Andreessen, venture capitalist*

My idea would not have been implemented and made part of the core FT business model just one year after it was born if the CCO and CEO had not been committed to it.

Internal champions higher in the hierarchy are essential, as I've said. They need to see the project as their baby, and they need to say, "I want to see this happen." Once people say they can do something, they naturally want to follow it through and make it happen successfully. Motivation structures work in both directions, at the bottom and the top. Management needs something new to be excited about; intrapreneurial minds live for something new. Moreover, to be effective, intrapreneurs need to ask for feedback from someone who believes in their vision as much as them – because they feel it belongs to them too.

Intrapreneurs have an above-average organisational bond: they feel they are making the company evolve, but they also recognise they can do this only thanks to the trust the company is placing in them.

Negotiation is a fundamental skill in any job. But intrapreneurs need it intrinsically: they have to negotiate for the idea initially, as they need to 'sell' to their superiors and generally their company that a corporate innovation project is worth the risk. Moreover, for the implementation of the idea pitched, they have to trade for resources (time and financial ones), which can be scarce owing to competing projects within the company.

When asking for resources, it should be clear to intrapreneurs how companies are structured when it comes to innovation budgets. Follow-

ing Brad Power and Steve Stanton's research (2014), corporate money
and resources go in four buckets. Allocating different amounts to each
bucket means positioning the company differently across the spectrum of
today/tomorrow innovation and impact:

1. Daily Operations: the operations executed within the stable operating model.
2. Incremental Improvement: the ongoing improvement projects that
   drive better efficiency and effectiveness within the existing management and organisational structure.
3. Sustaining Innovation: "by modifying the operating model or
   crossing internal boundaries", a meaningful change is enhanced.
   It requires a remarkable management structure within the existing
   hierarchies of the organisation, as it uses the current value network
   and considers current users/customers to address the innovation to.
4. Disruptive Innovation: this is a new venture fund. It needs research
   and development, incubation and a sort of protection. It happens in
   an autonomous unit, it looks for growth in a new market with new
   players and it is addressed to a new group of customers. It is classi-
   fied as a "significant breakthrough in the organisation's operating
   model and value network".

Intrapreneurs might act in all these four areas, but their most innovative
projects tap into the fourth bucket. However, this area is given the least
resources – so this is why, again, negotiation is critical.

In their research, Power and Staton find that the significant investments go to the first bucket (nearly 85% of resources go to day-to-day
operations, and only 5% on sustaining innovations and 5% to disruptive
innovations). However, when asking various managers how they would
improve the allocation, they immediately answered with a double per-
centage for innovation (10% for the third bucket, 10% for the fourth):
"organisations instinctively feel (and know) they should be spending
more" in creating the new.

From a holistic organisational perspective, top management knows
that to assure disruptive innovation success, they need to create a protected and autonomous area, with its own budgets and resources team.
And this is the space, the 'garden', in which an intrapreneur can act. If
this space is not there, intrapreneurs, through their own initiative, will

gain attention and demonstrate their impact in order to request an autonomous space.

Knowing these dynamics, you should leverage them when studying and then pitching your corporate innovation project (and, perhaps, strategy).

"Rather than realizing that managing the present and inventing the future are equally important and should be equally resourced, they often fight for the same resources. Often the execution engine deprives the innovators from access to valuable resources, like customers, brand, or skills. That means the innovators end up competing without any competitive advantage against the more nimble and agile startups"
*Steve Blank, a Silicon Valley serial-entrepreneur and expert on corporate innovation*

We have said that winning the support of the top management is key for any intrapreneur action and plan.

However, some of you might have felt or will feel that your ideas get killed not because they have low potential but because your boss or the people you are presenting them to do not understand them or, in the worst scenario, they do not even listen to your presentation.

I have learned from experience that you need to bring on board the people who will need to approve your idea as early as possible, way before you are in front of them pitching a solution to a problem.

Top executives are very busy and time-poor. And then, by default, their answer is no (Steve Jobs was the same!). Why?

Typically, most of them perceive the creation and testing of new ideas as a task to be executed by a small group of subordinates or external consultants – as we have already explored, these are the two routes for corporate practice innovation. However, we all know that only through the support of leaders 'getting out of the building' can innovative acts impact and have relevance in the business – and they can help make things move faster. So top executives have to be "more than just sponsors of new business ideas", as Alexander Osterwalder, the 'Business Model Generation' writer, said (in Steve Blank, 2016:2).

However, executives give negative responses to unexpected breakthroughs, even if you are talking to the best promoter of innovation within your company. This is because disruptive projects and ideas "require deep understanding and may have risky implications for the business. In such a situation, they, of course, prefer to say 'no'", says Roberto Verganti, Leadership and Innovation professor at Harvard Business School and

Stockholm Business School – with whom I had the pleasure of discussing this matter.

Knowing that, what is the antidote?

In a nutshell: even if you already have a new solution for answering a business problem/challenge/question, do not immediately pitch it.

It would be best to make the top executives part of your journey from the beginning of your innovation process.

Start with the business problem. It all begins with a question people are asked or are asking to solve. Start by researching the question more, as we do at university for our dissertation. Ask the right questions. It all starts with the hypothesis, on which you need to base your thesis theme and discussion. Investigate it and ask for time to look into the problem. You will likely get a 'yes' as an answer.

Then, with this initial support, it is your job to keep people engaged in the matter. Give them updates and feedback on the progress of your research. Give them essential information but not the overall picture. What you are doing here is pursuing radical innovation: not selling the idea, but selling the process.

As Homer said, "Evil deeds do not prosper; the slow man catches up with the swift." More time spent early on finding the root cause of a problem and doing good analytical research can save money for the system. Being 'slow' in your data-driven analysis and solution selection can reduce the risk that your idea will be killed later (and money will be wasted and, above all, you will lose the trust that was placed in you). This is why involving them in the process is critical.

What about persuasion? How to persuade them to be part of your project?

When chatting to serial intrapreneur Robin Kwong (now Newsroom Innovation Chief for the *Wall Street Journal*), he said the top skill for an intrapreneur is bringing clarity. Clarity on the problem you are trying to solve and why you are doing it, what you are expecting out of this business issue, and then communicating it.

Moreover, when you innovate, you need to make clear to the team and executives you are working with that you are not trying to change the company all in one go – as already discussed, we know their answer will be 'no'. As well, be clear with yourself: you do not have to convince 100 people: make sure you have understood and studied (active listening, as we said) who the three to five people are who can/need to say yes (and who are the other people who will say no – and why).

When you feel ready, involve the small group in creating the solution – and stop thinking about it as 'your' project. Robin Kwong said to me, "I always make my colleagues lead and work with me on the next innovation. Welcoming someone in is key for impact in any project I have ever developed."

This is how he approached one of his most successful ideas, the Uber Game of 2017, which became one of the most-read pieces of journalism published by FT in that year and a visual journalism success that garnered many awards. The project involved a small team made by a heterogeneous group of journalists, designers and developers. They were called to set up an interactive game in which the players act as a full-time Uber driver. Their wish was to make users critically reflect upon the constraints of such a job at Uber within other gig-economy platforms.

The result has been tremendous. Not only has the public response been unprecedented, but it has also turned out to be an educational resource. Next Gen Personal Finance, a non-profit that helps young people manage their money, created a worksheet for its students to reflect on their virtual experience of the Uber Game and related it to personal finance, showing that great interactive content can turn into an educational hub.

The game also brought new possibilities for exploring ways of creating content and applying storytelling to journalism within the company. No matter what happens next, what is important here is the impact on participants' lives and careers. Kwong indeed acted like an entrepreneur, but the important thing is that he made his team feel like a team of intrapreneurs, not working for someone, but with someone, to create something new.

As Verganti suggests in his leadership studies on this matter, Kwong made the "executives feel they own the idea".[1] So this means your idea will benefit from the precious insights of senior leaders – who have a unique perspective on the market owing to their experience – and more substantial support, as that innovative idea is their 'baby' too.

Many of you might argue, OK, then my boss will put his or her name on the project. Here we go again.

---

[1] You can find the article at: https://hbr.org/2010/08/how-to-sell-an-idea-to-your-bo.

I don't think this is entirely true. If you're lucky enough, you will get more support and, as your manager is part of the innovation process rather than the final idea (that you have already projected), it will be difficult for him/her to have complete ownership of the final product/project without involving you.

However, as a natural entrepreneur and intrapreneur, you should be ready to sacrifice your ego sometimes for the sake of innovation.

Another point in your favour as an intrapreneur is that you should be a good negotiator – so you should negotiate your branding on the idea you have developed.

**You belong to the seat you have been assigned to: reframing impostor syndrome**

> "When the beginner is aware of his needs, he ends up to be more clever than the absent-minded wise"
> *Paulo Coelho*

I talked about listening, learning before doing. But we are also here to discuss how many younger people have great ideas which really do change a company or an industry.

And if you are given trust as an intrapreneur, you might find yourself managing or leading someone older than yourself.

More than three in five Millennial employees (62%) and 49% of Gen Z employees say they have line managers (direct reports), according to the March 2020 Zapier data report.[2]

First point: you belong to the seat you have been assigned to. Don't worry about other people's roles – think about what your role is. If the role is leading a group, do not feel bad about it. Push back your insecurities, hold on to what the job asks you to do. You got picked because of your talent and skill set.

Competence is not correlated with age.

If some colleagues openly attribute competence to age, this is how 'ageism' looks like, and it is discrimination.

---

[2] https://zapier.com/blog/millennial-managers-report/ and https://zapier.com/blog/digital-natives-report/.

However, Jodi Glickman – author of *Great on the Job* – wrote that the two extreme dynamics we might see in these circumstances are: the emerging generation feel the senior one is "not getting it" and kind of "standing in the way"; at the same time, the senior leaders question the relevance of the tech-savvy/innovative newcomer.

Both the positions are wrong and are based on biases and stereotypes.

Plutarch believed that the major obstacle in learning from others is one's own limitations and insecurities.

As this book is written by a younger generation representative (I am a 1993 girl), this is what I have learned when I found myself having a direct relationship with more experienced colleagues – sometimes managing them – and wanted both of us to benefit from our work relationship. This circumstance will happen to you often if you find yourself in an intrapreneurial role. This is what I have learnt.

## 1. *Stop legitimising yourself*

Stop questioning yourself too much. Be grounded when you talk about your ideas. Ground your concept in a familiar little twist, and you will encounter less resistance. However, do not justify yourself too much for what you are doing. If you lead that project, that is your job. Some extroverts might be born with it, but confidence is not in all of us by default. You can build it over time. It might be of great help to ask for mentorship from someone who might have faced the same – as we will discuss soon.

## 2. *Reframe self-doubt: embrace feedback and cross-mentoring*

Let's touch on another critical phenomenon that might affect you at this stage of your career: the imposter syndrome. We can define this as the persistent chronic thought that tells you that you do not deserve your accomplishments. I have often experienced this, and I believe many of you have. Many psychologists suggest reframing self-doubt and turning it into something more constructive and productive. In "How to Make Friends with Your Inner Imposter", Amantha Imber suggests we should see self-doubt as a humble attitude to be channelled into a mindset of "this is an opportunity for me to learn".[3]

---

[3] You can find the article at: https://hbr.org/2021/05/how-to-make-friends-with-your-inner-imposter.

However, we should always consider point one: you belong to the seat you have been assigned to.

If this is an attitude to apply to our inner conversations, this is also applicable to our external world's confrontations. Open to learning, but with personality.

The only way to grow as a person and professional is to know what we are doing wrong. No one likes it, but it is critical for our personal growth.

Vulnerability is a great activity to build credibility: find people who can help you in a few different ways and ask for help. However, being over-confident might be irritating for some senior leaders – as they might feel they are not of any use.

Once I pitched a project to a very senior leader, and she did not even listen to the idea itself, but my assertive approach made her give me this feedback: "I don't know why you are here to ask my opinion on your project if you are so confident about it."

You can imagine how I felt: I was there to ask her for help in making the project happen.

I learnt that a younger person's maturity comes out of openly talking about their vulnerability: start with the reasons behind your project but make it clear from the beginning that you want to involve that senior leader in the process – and that you need them. Acknowledge your limitations, what you need to improve, and ask for help. Faking complete confidence in your idea will damage your trustworthiness as you will look like a cocky kid. This, even if it comes out of the best intentions, intensely annoys a senior leader.

Oppositely, keep your attitude away from deference. That is a firm no go: the most counterproductive thing you can do. It will only create distance and formality. What you want out of this cross-mentoring experience is to be a transformational opportunity for both of you: learning something new and helping each other. As Carucci writes (2020), "deference triggers a sense of imposter syndrome, a fear many older leaders have (that they aren't worthy of the role they are in)".[4] This shows that you can encounter this psychological phenomenon at different stages of your career life.

---

[4] You can find the article at: https://hbr.org/2020/10/build-a-relationship-with-a-senior-leader-you-admire.

Additionally, a mistake will not mark you forever: do not take negative feedback personally but frame it as an opportunity. Above all, the person giving you feedback invested time to do so and does that to see you learn and improve – and believe you can, as Imber writes.

You should always ask for feedback and open a direct dialogue with the senior colleague. The experience of your senior co-worker can only help you to improve your project. As an intrapreneur, your role is to make decisions, bring a team of different people together (who never worked together before!), influence others and get your vision started. As my manager said to me once, "sometimes the question isn't 'is there something wrong?' but instead 'could it be better?'" – and innovative and visionary projects can always be better. Therefore, feedback is key.

Setting up a healthy working relationship with a senior colleague will help you progress your career (not just your project). Before getting to work, it is good practice to create a positive working environment with any colleague, but I think it is a must if you have more senior people involved. Spend some time getting to know each other and establish a 'feedback time' to increase efficiency and transparency. In fact, we can have a healthy work environment only through cross-mentoring. To be a complete professional, as a young leader, you need to inherit the wisdom of those who came before you. More senior leaders can build their legacy only if they mentor the younger ones to reach their full potential. They have authority, and you can only learn from them as a junior employee.

It's a two-way conversation, understanding the wants and needs of both and their different perspectives. Corporations need to work on bridging the gap between the two groups, building a bridge. Co-workers can start exercising empathy, trying to walk in each other's shoes to understand certain attitudes better. The value of this attitude is immense because it allows learning from more experienced co-workers while broadening your network within the organisation – and it can build your own 'gravitas'.

### 3. *Use the human factor*

When it comes to building a new working relationship with someone more experienced than you, start with the human factor: you are both humans. Use your empathic and emotional intelligence to understand better who is in front of you and neutralise the hierarchy difference between you and the interlocutor.

Use your radar to see what might be the common ground between you and that person – and, as I learnt, most of the time you can find this outside work. And a more senior colleague taught me this.

Once I was meant to be working with a board member. I was very nervous about it. However, this colleague, who knew how to play very well with empathy, intercepted my anxiety and started talking about his experiences and passion for music. When I found out his first job was in the music industry, I noticed that our shared passion for music built another ground for our working relationship. We shared something outside the single project and the working ecosystem – and it was deeply human, as music can be. We established mutuality, setting a common human ground, leading to a solid and healthy relationship. Of course, don't make the senior interlocutor feel you have been spying on them before your meeting, but do show a genuine interest in what they do as a human, not just as a professional.

However, don't ignore the hierarchy differences between you – and be respectful about it, always showing you are eager to learn from their experiences.

### 4. *Aim to build a great innovative team*

When any person from any part of your organisation comes into your working project, you need to create a healthy and exciting working environment. To build innovation is all about the people, we said. Therefore, the spirit you are bringing within your team is fundamental to create long-lasting relationships within your corporation, especially with more senior colleagues.

It would be best if you had these four critical aspects developed in your 'aura', the atmosphere that people enter into when working with you:

- A constant wave of enthusiasm around new projects.
- As an intrapreneur, you need to be results-driven and avoid at all costs the effect of an 'innovation lab'. Ideas must be followed by actions.
- Give a sense of belonging: the more the team feels part of something new and unique, the more attached to the project it will be.
- Reward dedication: smaller teams, made by people totally involved in the process, push their dedication to the project. Choosing this

structure, rather than big teams of people partially involved in the process, increases the level of dedication and enthusiasm.

## Reverse ageism: let's talk about age discrimination

"Be persevering at the bottom, humble at the top"
*Maxime Lagace*

Age discrimination, also known as ageism, is the most prevalent form of prejudice experienced by older and younger people. This is why corporate strategies for reducing age prejudice must address ageism as a multigenerational challenge.

Many intrapreneurs will know what I am talking about here when I say 'reverse ageism': when younger professionals face prejudice and discrimination because of their age, often under the form of patronising stereotypes when it comes to trust, employability, feedback in the workplace.

At the same time, it is essential to underline that older employees face bias because of their age, especially in some industries. Technology is at the top of the list. One example: a ProPublica 2018 investigation by Gosselin and Tobin on IBM's cutting of tens of thousands of US workers, "hitting its most senior employees hardest, flouting rules against age bias". However, legislation comes in, offering laws and regulations to prevent ageism against 40+ workers (for example, in the USA, the federal Age Discrimination in Employment Act, or ADEA (29 USC § § 621–634), is the primary federal law that forbids employers from age discrimination against employees and applicants who are at least 40 years old; the European Commission has been addressing this since 2000).

It is not quite the same with younger employees – there is no clear legislation around that (Waldman, 2020), even though younger employees (52% of ages 18–34) are more likely than older employees (39% of ages 55+) to have witnessed or experienced ageism at work, as the Glassdoor diversity and inclusion survey in the UK, France, Germany and USA shows.

Therefore, companies play a role in protecting all generations: discrimination can take multiple forms and varies on a personal level, but corporations can work on intergenerational cohesion and resource distribution between ages – and make people more aware of the processes and the different positions at each age stage.

I would love to give you some practical examples here of how to tackle reverse ageism if you ever face it. From personal experience, I know many southern European colleagues face it quite brightly and openly in their workspaces – where reverse ageism is an openly neglected problem: ageism has a lot to do with each country's socio-political setup. For example, if you live "in a country with stronger structural support for older people, younger people are more likely to suffer age discrimination" (see the research of Bratt, Abrams and Swift from 2020 – which analyses data from 29 EU countries).

We talked about journalism as being a Janus. It means we need a bridge between tradition and change, and connecting between different skill sets as much as between different generations has never been more critical. So for the news industry, it is fundamental to build a transformational path with transferable skills in both directions for the more traditional part of the business – e.g. writing, reporting, analysis, and for the emerging – now even embedded – side, the technological one – e.g. data, multi-platforms, formats). This is why cross-mentoring is vital, as we noted earlier.

Reverse ageism builds walls rather than bridges for mutual learning. When an older worker questions the competency of a younger colleague, it is a double-edged sword against themselves and the overall organisation. Mistrust and biased assumptions will be used then across the board (the younger saying from now on "I cannot talk to this person from this group as they do not get it"; the older thinking "I cannot trust this person as they cannot lead this kind of tasks").

I understand people can easily distrust those who have less work experience than themselves. I do. Once I entered my first meeting with a director from a potential client company and, even though I was the project lead, I was asked to take notes; I was automatically by default the secretary – while the real team admin was assumed to be the manager, because of our age difference. I know this was not done with bad intent but came out of a common bias assumption.

Here are a few antidotes to reverse ageism we can adopt as younger employees.

*Use your age as one of your assets*

You belong to a different generation that is, most of the time, the future or present customer generation that has to be reached. You kind of 'know better' by default as you belong to it. Don't let the discrimination make you doubt yourself: if you were hired, you belong to the seat you were assigned to, as we said. So use your competitive advantage in response to any ageism situation. Make clear your point of view comes out of your experience, too: you might not have the same years of experience in the job, but you have a user perspective experience, a personal pragmatic one – that can be equally valuable. You might know more about younger generations' languages and communications, formats, things you know would work with a particular audience – the one you belong to! This is quite strategic in the news industry, which, as we explored, needs the younger generation to be part of the innovations within the media. Or you might use examples that come out of an experience you know more about (e.g. "as a Gen Z myself, I have seen my peers using this kind of product in this way ... it worked well for this campaign...").

*Build your network*

Ask for the support of younger colleagues and mentors. Sharing your experience with someone facing the same hurdles or who has lived them in the past is beneficial. It is crucial to share insights and see how someone is facing similar obstacles and doubts (or what they did about them).

*Empower the younger people in the room*

You will find yourself in the situation where there is someone even younger than you in the meeting. And you will remember just a few months or years before being in that same uncomfortable situation. So it is your turn to be the person you hoped was there in that room with you. Try to facilitate the interaction of the younger colleague with the group and be the kind of person you wished you had in those same circumstances. Once you know this person's skills, be confident and clear in making the team aware of these capabilities and be open in showing that they know what they are doing. Give them opportunities to challenge themselves and shine, be their sponsor.

Give back again is our mantra here.

# 17    Wabi-sabi and the 'blisters' career approach

"Whatever decision you have made for your future, you are authorized, and I would say encouraged, to subject it to continuous scrutiny, ready to change it, if it no longer responds to your wishes"
*Rita Levi Montalcini*

It would be natural to think of our career as a linear process, driven by a simple rule: if you work hard, then you obtain results. However, real life is non-linear. Whether you're starting a career or learning the bass, understanding and embracing non-linear progress is the only way to stay motivated through the challenges you could face. Especially at the beginning, your business life could be imperfect; you could find reaching goals and concretising dreams hard. You could be forced to do something that you do not really fit with, accept duties that you do not really like or go back to study something completely new. It is beautiful, and it is challenging. Your career path looks more like a Jackson Pollock painting than a Giotto one. It seems like something that the Japanese would call 'wabi-sabi'.

The Japanese culture calls 'wabi-sabi' a beauty that is "imperfect, impermanent, and incomplete". Richard Powell, in his book *Wabi Sabi Simple* (2004) wrote that "Wabi-sabi nurtures all that is authentic by acknowledging three simple realities: nothing lasts, nothing is finished, and nothing is perfect" (Powell 2004).[1] The personalised texture creates our own beauty that we have earned through the journey: the same can be applied to your career path.

The beginning of your career is an integral part of your life trip. And it does not mean that you will not have activities that you do not entirely

---

[1] Richard Powell, *Wabi Sabi Simple* (Adams Media, 2004).

appreciate when you are in a more senior position. It might be a budget review, a report to write, some admin hiring processes. However, there is an exciting point that professor of organisational behaviour at London Business School Dan Cable explains in his HBR article "What You Should Follow Instead of Your Passion". He sees a more helpful career approach in "follow your blisters" rather than "follow your passion". How many times have we been advised to follow what you are passionate about? On average, we spend more than one-third of our entire life at work. So your job definitely has a significant impact on your quality of life – and we should be spending that one-third of our life doing something we enjoy.

But let's be honest. We will never be able to find the perfect job, basically because it does not exist. Every job has its own nuances, ups and downs – even the intrapreneur's job. But also, you as a person have your own capabilities and skill set. Specifically, if you are an intrapreneur, you have a particular range of pretty good soft skills. However, nobody is perfect, right? You might be very good at something in your job but have other tasks that you find a bit more complicated.

For me, it is writing in a foreign language. Maybe because I am too in love with my Italian, I find it challenging to be as expressive as I would be in my mother tongue, especially when writing.

When I was doing my first work experience in London as a graduate scheme trainee, one of the directors told me after six months of my collaboration, "Virginia, I know you are passionate about this industry, but you will never be working with your accent in the news." Discrimination besides – that is not the point here – I remember it was one of the most frustrating moments of my life. But I knew the guy was right. My English was not perfect (it still isn't!), and if I wanted to be a professional working abroad, I needed to improve it. But it is still not my best skill; I don't have a complete "use of English" – I miss some jokes, I don't know many different popular expressions, and I don't get some accents from certain regions when people talk too fast.

That is a blister. Wow, and a big one. It took me so much energy to be 24/7 speaking in English, and I invested a lot of my time to be ready for that.

But this senior colleague gave me a big push to improve myself, and here I am writing my first book in English. I improved myself, trying to take any opportunity I could in my job to be writing and speaking. I tried to be the same person I was while speaking in another language: trying to talk as much as possible with my colleagues, asking them to correct me, to help me improve. Fear is what holds us back – also, fear of asking for help and being vulnerable shows what it means to be humble. Taking risks is the only way to improve ourselves. Generating blisters and following them means finding an area we will always be learning about.

"So, if you're looking to find a career that will matter to you, instead of looking only in the direction of 'passion,' also think about the activities that you return to – despite the fact that they are harder to complete than things you are more immediately or emotionally drawn to", Cable writes (2020).[2] Whatever it is, the crucial point here, especially when you're starting your career journey as many of this book's readers are, is to follow your blisters as your keys for continuous learning. This is the only way to be an 'expert': "When you practice an activity a bit more obsessively than other people, you build a unique character – you earn some wear and some healing that makes you idiosyncratic and a little unbalanced" (ibid.).

You will never be perfect at your job, especially if you tend to be curious and explore different areas as an intrapreneurial individual does. But you will become progressively more expert in specific parts, building a unique asset for you as a professional. Take risks, make mistakes and find areas where you can constantly improve. You will never get bored.

Some of you already know what you want to be at school, and you have passed straight from a traditional academic career within top-level universities. Others will have jumped from one path to another to reach the same goals. That's fine. In the last ten years, I've learned that nothing is more authentic and accurate than your instinct. Trust it and let it guide you to see the best strategic plan for reaching a possible point (which is not definite but ever-evolving as you learn and change as a professional). I started at home, from piles of fresh newspapers with the morning coffee. I have experienced reporting as a freelance journalist, I studied cultural economy, then Media and Communication with a sociology perspective. Even within the *Financial Times* my path has not been vertical but looks more like a z-shaped one. The truth is that I never believed that I should be driven by what I want to achieve in the future, but by what I want to

---

[2] https://hbr.org/2020/11/what-you-should-follow-instead-of-your-passion.

learn in the present – so as to be ready for the future. If observed from this perspective, your career run looks more like a trail than a marathon. You never know which obstacles and difficulties you will have to face and where your feet will bring you, but it does not matter because you are not focused on the finish line but on your track. Learning the value of every experience, change, transferable skill and failure makes you a quick-learning individual who can become an extremely valuable professional capable of adapting to new environments and challenging situations. Do everything without fear. You will never regret it.

# 18    Younger talent and the news industry: FT Talent Challenge and give back leadership

"Pleasure in the job puts perfection in the work"
Aristotle

My first intrapreneur's experiment, FT Talent Challenge, matched my interest in the news with my willingness to attract younger and entrepreneurial people in an industry – to change it from within, with the human factor. When I first thought about it, my wish was to create something that could make a difference, something happening now but lasting into the future and impacting our society and our company. As we said, innovation starts with the people.

I still remember how joyful I was when I first saw FT Talent take place in 2018. When I saw 50 students from the most diverse parts of the world entering the FT, and I noticed the same happiness shared by the fantastic group of colleagues all working together and making this possible. We were so tired, from the most diverse age groups, blowing up balloons that had just been delivered. That is when I realised something different was happening: a group of total strangers believed in my vision and they were having fun. I will never forget the happiness that I felt. It was something like being on a high mountain, hiking and feeling dizzy – but in a very exciting way.

FT Talent Challenge is a programme that brings together students and early career professionals (the 'challengers') driven by proactivity and curiosity in a competition that takes part in the *Financial Times* headquarters around the world. The aim is to challenge the FT ecosystem and assumptions on the future of news and other industries.

The talent selected is not the 'usual' FT prospect reader (business school students, future consultants or banking professionals, etc.), because we want to reach new groups of potential readers who have never heard of our newspaper or never connected with financial news. Diversity in terms of social background and studies is what we look for primarily.

Every person is immersed in one ecosystem, inheriting social and economic conditions that they did not choose. These pre-conditions can be difficult to climb and surpass.

At the beginning of your career, you tend not to consider a few elements that can count meaningfully in shaping your journey in the job market. When looking at career start and then progression the social background and 'social class' you come from, the place where you were born, the exposure to culture and stimuli, the path you have been involved in through your family journey – and the people involved and met on that journey: this all weighs on your future and perspective.

This means the recurrent philosophy "if you want it, you can do it" it is not feasible for many people out there. This is why corporations – especially media groups, which should represent and enable democratic actions (as we said in Chapter 1) – have the opportunity (but also the duty) to open up opportunities and be a channel for people to scale the economic ladder. First, by being a tool for empowerment, a quality information provider can offer news and education to people who did not have enough support to be educated. This means not just offering the product but presenting it, reaching new and diverse audiences, and making clear the relevance that being informed can have in your life (from financial literacy for your investment or savings decisions, to a political perspective allowing you to become an informed citizen and voter, etc.) Secondly, a news entity can be a connector, offering networking opportunities through its brand and platform to rebalance the social disequilibrium that economic and ethnographic backgrounds (and generally the structure of our society) can play in someone's future. It means using the channels of a powerful media to bring under the spotlight not the usual talent and to give other voices an opportunity to shine and be discovered (telling their stories, listening to their constructive criticism and feedback, building a meaningful relationship).

Alignment of circumstances, goodwill, talent but also luck play a significant role in shaping your career.

We cannot forget about luck and that 'door opener' moment I experienced. Without an alignment of circumstances – a 'free' moment of a leader, a willingness to be open to dialogue (maybe because in that week there was no other urgent matter that made our meeting get postponed or cancelled, as happened to me many other times, or because there was a sense of urgency about customer feedback: I will never know...) – I would not be in the same position as I am today. Maybe I would have done something similar and would have got there thanks to my strategic thinking and way of looking at the job market, and also my cultural privilege (that needs to be admitted but also not blamed), but I definitely would not have had the precious and quick ladder-scaling opportunity I had when I was just 22 years old.

With FT Talent we try to attract those talented people who may not think about the media industry as a potential workplace: engineers, coders, data scientists – and people without a specific background but with demonstrated talent. Normally, they look for tech giants and startups as innovation hubs or have no idea where to start their career – the news industry is not perceived as a potential workplace for these profiles. And yet the media industry is incurring a crucial transformation moment – and needs diverse talent to implement innovative strategies. Intrapreneurs, especially from different and heterogeneous backgrounds, are needed like air. Moreover, to truly be a global voice, you need to have an inclusive voice, representing the different communities and audiences whose perspectives you want to hear.

Let's take a step back. We have already mentioned the original sin, the run to the colonisation of the Internet that press companies made years ago, after the advent of the web. They are still exploring the same strategy now, through their strategies on social media. In this process, we assisted with what we can call an atomisation of the content, short and brief news, moulded by social media logics, and often optimised to catch our greed for news and updates. In it, we lost the 'morning prayer' that we have already mentioned, that moment of the day when the magic, the serendipity happened, and the reader had the chance to learn and critically think about the structured opinions and analysis provided by the press. This is something that only an audience-centred business model can provide, radically different from the logic of volumes that drive social media algorithms.

Millennials, but most of all Gen Z representatives, are the critical individuals to drive this run back to the audience instead of the content, and this is why they are at the core of the FT Talent Challenge, not only as principal actors, but also as part of the prospective FT audience.

They are the social generation, and they are likely to start their journey within the news from social media, rather than websites or apps. Instagram, Twitter, TikTok and Telegram groups are their primary resource, a sort of 'bridge' (I am borrowing the word from Caspar De Bono, FT's former B2B managing director) between what they learn in their classrooms and reality. Studying their behaviour and bringing their experience within the industry means fighting the side effects of the atomisation I mentioned before, keeping its potential to attract the attention of younger generations. To do this, high-quality content tailored to the audience is required. And who can produce better tailored content than someone from the audience itself?

Again, the power of payback comes to our attention. The company gives these new players the possibility to touch the news environment, to bring their talent and their feedback to the FT to give their fresh view on what we are doing as a company and media group. This is why the FT Talent Challenge is a model that works. In this sense, the programme could be seen as a talent incubator and as a massive resource for the media company to make the most of in order to thrive in the future – and connect with an audience that is willing to pay but needs to have a guide and a direction to choose its sources.

It is also an opportunity for me to give back the opportunity I received when Mr Slade offered me his time for my dissertation and, moreover, gave me a hint to think about the FT as a place to start a career in the news industry. Through FT Talent Challenge I can amplify that 'door opening' moment I received and give that opportunity to see the media world as approachable to as many talented individuals as possible – younger talent, most of whom come from unprivileged or different backgrounds or experiences. However, they are in the same room as a board member and another student of the same age from Oxbridge.

# 19　Diverse is beautiful: diversity and inclusion in the news system

"The future cannot be predicted, but futures can be invented"
*Dennis Gabor*

## Diversity matters (and wins!)

Diversity and inclusion are not just two beautiful (and beneficial PR/marketing) concepts, but they are the real sparkling duo that create a vibrant environment rich with different perspectives and backgrounds.

Diversity refers to a full spectrum of different ages, religions, races, sexual orientations, genders, skill sets and experiences.

Inclusion means making everyone in this varied group feel involved, valued, respected, treated fairly and embedded in the culture. It also means empowering any part of this group and creating a more inclusive company. Without diversity and inclusion, any company's workforce risks feeling out of place and unsupported.

Adopting diversity and inclusiveness within the business model creates more adaptable and creative work environments, but most of all it is attractive for top talents. The data in the "Why Diversity Matters" 2015 McKinsey report shows that organisations with significant ethnic diversity are 35% more likely to outperform their competitors, while with every 10% increase in gender diversity, EBIT (earnings before interest and taxes) increases by 3.5%. Moreover, businesses that are in the top quartile for racial, ethnic and gender diversity have a 25% greater likelihood of being more profitable than the national median for their respective industry.

Another point should be considered about the generational shift. By 2025 Millennials will make up 75% of the global workforce. This will have a substantial impact on the way inclusion and diversity will be seen in the workplace. Millennials differ from the former generation because they consider diversity to be a mix of experience, identities, ideas and opinions. Older generations perceive diversity in terms of equality, representation of demographic characteristics and religion (Deloitte, 2015). The former group associates the concept of inclusion with using collaborative tools to drive business impact, the latter with acceptance, integration and tolerance. The difference is enormous.

In an industry like the news, the hot issue is stimulating innovation and digital disruption while remaining competitive. Globalisation and technology are considered nowadays to be drivers of performance. Research shows that if we consider their impact on the relationship between diversity and performance, we can observe that societies with the most emphasis on digital innovation have the highest level of impact made by diversity. Moreover, the relationship between diversity and innovation is stronger for companies with interests and operations in multiple countries.

This is what we are building through the FT Talent Challenge project and many more initiatives to amplify the base from which we can expand our brand and meaning. Only through similar projects can we be a truly global and inclusive 2020s voice.

## Journalism and diversity

A 2016 report, "Journalists in the UK" by Dr Neil Thurman, Dr Alessio Cornia and Dr Jessica Kunert, analyses trends and perspectives from over 700 UK journalists surveyed.

Data shows that journalism is quite behind in reaching inclusive representation: the diversity problem in terms of ethnicity is significant.

Comparing the survey results with data from the 2011 UK Census shows a notable under-representation of journalists from ethnic backgrounds when compared with the UK population. The most under-represented group are Black Britons who are under-represented by a factor of more than ten. They are then followed by Asian Britons (representing approximately 7% of the UK population but just 2.5% of the 700 journalists surveyed) (see Figure 7).

*Figure 7*   Ethnicity of non-white UK journalists in 2015

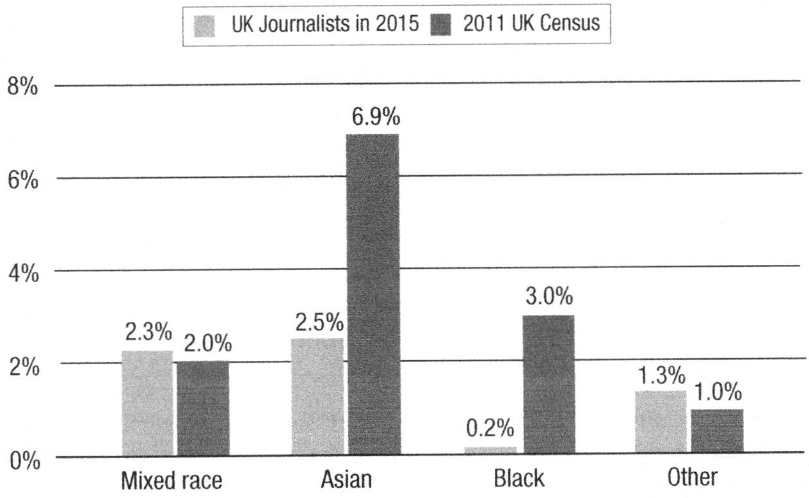

*Source*: elaboration on data from Reuters 2016.

The persistent failure to reach even moderate levels of ethnic diversity in journalism means that not all of the population have their voices represented. This is why there is an urgency for projects such as FT Talent Challenge to turn into the norm.

I was pretty impressed to find in the report the testimony of a Muslim magazine editor, who said "ethnicity had been a hindrance" when applying for jobs. So much so that he once "applied for the same job using an 'English' sounding name and got an interview after being rejected the first time" (page 13).

As we have noted before, getting into journalism is highly competitive: it requires "either a lot of luck or someone you know" (personal communication noted in Reuters report, February 2016: 13). This is, sadly, still true (and not just in the UK, of course). In fact, in the interviews conducted, it emerged that social connection is one of the main ways to get a career into journalism – meaning that immigrants and their relatives (mainly their daughters and sons) are prevented from getting into the industry as they do not have the relevant connections.

The lack of diversity starts early when students graduate and begin their professional journey as part of the journalism workforce.

The probability of journalism students being employed as a journalist six months after graduation oscillates quite a lot if analysed under the diversity lens: the report shows that white students have a 26% chance, while black students only have an 8% chance; male students have 29% chance, while female students have a 24% chance; privately funded students have a 25% chance, while state-funded students have a 17% chance.

The diversity percentages in journalism could be undoubtedly changed if media organisations keep and extend inclusive schemes as much as developing innovative streams of non-academic journalism/alternative candidates, such as modern apprenticeships and work experiences within the news group (such as FT Talent, a flexible entry point programme that can be easily imitated by other news and media groups to increase their diversity).

From the leadership and talent acquisition side, being conscious and addressing current selection bias issues is vital to meaningfully changing the future of the media.

*Mulier nova*

Before closing this book, I believe it is necessary, as a young woman, to briefly touch on the gender question: what does it mean to work in the news for a woman under 30?

Luba Kassova, Co-Founder and Director of AKAS, authored the two "Missing Perspectives in News" reports in 2020, which the Bill & Melinda Gates Foundation commissioned.

It focuses on how much women's voices have been cut out from the coverage of the COVID-19 crisis.

The result is surprising (and not in a positive way), especially considering that women have been the group most impacted by the pandemic – and the lifestyle connected to the lockdown. The report aimed to provide a picture of how women interact with news and provide ideas on reaching them with valuable and tailored content, genuinely reflecting their wishes and needs. The questions from the report are still open.

A story can guide our thinking in this area and provide solutions to the report's questions.

Academy Award-winning actor Geena Davis, while watching them with her daughter, noticed that the protagonists of films and cartoons were predominantly male and started wondering if movie production was influenced by unconscious bias. Therefore, in 2007, she founded the Geena Davis Institute of Gender in Media and, partnered with Google, developed a GD-IQ tool to collect data in films indicating potential gender bias. In the following decade, the Institute shared their findings with producers, directors and actors, discovering many motion picture studios that wanted to reduce the gender gap within their productions. Filling the gap would not only have been beneficial for the audience, but also for the studios: the smaller the gap, the wider the reachable public.

Something similar happened at the FT. Back in 2017, according to female customers' feedback, there were too many suits on the home page – meaning that the paper was not seen as approachable by a female reader because there was no fit and no female representation, even from just an iconographic perspective. As we know since prehistoric times, images, paintings, sculptures and indeed any form of representation has a mirroring and familiarity effect on the viewer. Since the male predominance was not representative of the company's aimed readership (with no gender bias), JanetBot became the new product idea that could help the company to reduce this bias. It was a simple AI tool to quantify the volume of male images compared with female ones on every page of the paper: if not enough women were represented, an 'alarm' would signal this to the newsroom, so action could be taken before going online. Again, the presence of women appears not only a diverse and inclusive choice, but also a compulsory one to drive business impact: four years later female readership has drastically improved and, moreover, many more initiatives are running to make FT Women a more impactful part for our news business (which means it increases subscriber numbers, which is then beneficial to our business model).

When it comes to an infrastructural analysis of the journalism market, from the same 2016 Reuters report on UK Journalists we mentioned before, data shows that there is a substantial surge of women into journalism (they make up 45% of the news workforce now); moreover, they form a majority among young journalists. However, they are less well remunerated and are under-represented in senior positions as they get stuck in junior management roles. Consequently, this results in fewer female journalists having the liberty to select news stories, decide which aspects of the news should be stressed and which people should be featured – and have a say in editorial decision-making processes.

The sex ratio for the entire world population is 101 males to 100 females (2021 estimate, WHO Data). Women are literally half of the market out there. Not catching it means losing half of the cake. Women wish for products and contents to be designed also for them (not *just* for them), and to be gender-aware, putting them (too) at the centre of public and political discourse. They want to be seen, and represented, but this can happen only in an environment with spaces for them at all levels of decision-making. An environment, again, diverse and inclusive – and aware of diversity.

This tallies with Lucy Kueng's (2020) observations in her book on newsroom cultures: any media business model that requires financial and personal commitment from a reader must address the issue of diversity head on – even internally.

In other words, what women want is the news industry of the future. We are already operating in an environment where news is moving to mobile and to platforms. A newsroom that harnesses these changes also understands the need to change the culture of the newsroom to better reflect the needs of their audience.

# Conclusion

We opened this book with the *Allegory of the Cave* – one of Socrates' most famous myths – as a journey through enlightenment. How to get out of a dark cavern we are constantly immersed in, full of stimuli, lights, shadows and connections it is so difficult to make sense of?

This book wants to indicate which direction to take, not give final solutions. It is a view of what is critical nowadays and what is happening in the news ecosystem – especially on the human side.

We have travelled together through the complex world of the network, the role of intrapreneurs, what innovation means. We have explored the relationship between journalism and technology – where it is going and the potential mistakes and goals of its evolution.

Finding the balance between tradition and change, preserving the quality and the integrity of the journalistic activity while adapting to the new rhythm of the network is not an easy task. Therefore, analysing the daily dilemmas of practitioners, experimenting and engaging in an open and constructive conversation with other players as incumbents or entrants, is crucial. Moreover, it is fundamental to preserve the quality of the news as a piece of information and a moment of experience, deploying technologies as tools for quality's sake, with a long-term perspective.

No one has yet cracked the business model or the proper infrastructure that will sustain quality journalism in the next decades.

However, you could be the one who will crack it. You could be part of the intergenerational team required by the press industry to thrive in the future.

The essential attitude of this team should be working together for a quality news outlet and being committed to a standard shared value system that looks at journalism as a business but, above all, as a functional social actor essential for democracy and citizenship. This is the competitive advantage of quality that journalism has to leverage when rethinking its sustainability and role.

While doing that, news organisations need to reconnect to what people need from the news: a trustworthy, reliable, sense-making entity. Information needs audiences, and audiences need quality journalism. Specifically, the industry needs to connect to its prospective readers: the younger audience.

No one knows if traditional news publishers in the way we know them will survive the next 50 years – or if digital outlets and aggregating platforms will usurp their position. What is sure is that embracing disruption is the only way to go – and it is as fascinating as it is risky. This is why the role of young leading intrapreneurs has never been more vital, especially as they represent the younger audience group that news outlets need to talk to.

In this second part of the book, I hope any aspiring young game-changers, in big corporations and smaller companies, have found suggestions on how to leave a mark in their career journeys.

As a young woman manager in her 20s looking with an innovative entrepreneurial approach at a centenary business – the publishing one – my biggest wish is that this book can open a door (as much as the FT Talent Challenge programme idea) for further experiments and readings, and why not, for new disrupting projects and fresh opinions made by a new generation of intrapreneurs.

Because, yes, the news world is indeed one of the most challenging, intriguing and impactful industries to work in. And we are all waiting for you to take part in this transformational journey – and to make a real impact on our society.

# Afterword

It is sometimes said that journalists are curious about everything in the world except how they get paid. The traditional church-and-state barrier between editorial and business within news organisations has at times calcified into uninterest and apathy about the role and impact of business models within journalism. As Virginia Stagni writes in this charming and insightful book, that apathy is a luxury no longer afforded to an industry in crisis. Instead, she makes a persuasive case for fostering intrapreneurial leaders within news organisations, leaders able to chart a new and brighter future.

As the Founding CEO of Chartbeat, the default real-time analytics service used by publishers in 60 countries around the world, and subsequently as the Founder and CEO of Scroll (now the core of Twitter's new subscription business), I saw the challenges that Stagni elucidates close up. The news industry had already weathered the dollars-to-dimes move from print to digital and the accidental disruption of its lucrative classifieds business by the kindly and humble Craig Newmark of Craigslist. It then had to face new and overpowering competition in digital advertising from large platforms such as Google and Facebook, who swiftly took a majority share of ad spend. The industry problems outlined in the first half of this book are real and current.

For any other industry, we might look at this as just part of the cycle of life as companies and industries are disrupted by new innovations that replace them. However, journalism holds a special social importance that not all industries can aspire to. As Stagni says early on in this book: "Journalism does need democracy to exist and, everyone agrees, that democracy does need journalism".

So what to do? Drawing on her own personal story from her childhood within a family press agency in Bologna through to driving intrapreneurial efforts within the *Financial Times*, Stagni lays out a blueprint for how to grow and empower intrapreneurs to disrupt the industry from within before the job is done from without.

I've seen the power of intrapreneurial models at work within my own companies. At Chartbeat, we had a strong and dominant business within the analytics space. However, we could see the storm clouds engulfing the news industry as their business model was disrupted by the platforms and knew that we had to do something about it. We set up a separate team of intrapreneurs, identifying employees with vision and drive to tackle the problem and giving them the space and resources to get things done. While I was kept constantly in the loop on their developments, the team acted as an autonomous mini-startup within a larger company, making their own decisions and charting their own path.

That team was responsible for creating a wholly new way of measuring ad value, moving away from the tyranny of the click towards attention-based metrics that quantitatively linked the quality of the content to the value of the page. With a speed that was astounding even to me now, they built mechanisms for predicting, pacing, delivering, measuring and auditably reporting a brand new Cost-per-Hour metric that is still seen as cutting edge today.

If that team had not been given the kind of protected autonomous space, budget and resources that Stagni argues for, if they had not been able to act as 'diplomatic rebels' within a larger organisation they might still have created useful products but they would not have been so bold or their work so vital.

I highly encourage those within the ranks of media executives and beyond to take the lessons from this book and think deeply about the changes necessary within their organisations to see this intrapreneurial vision become a reality. It may involve turbulence and even a feeling of a loss of control, but the future we are fighting for is vital and we need to leverage every spark of creativity and drive within our industry to ensure that journalism has a thriving future. Building a new generation of intrapreneurs is key to that future and with this book Stagni shows the way.

*Tony Haile*

# Bibliography

## Part I

Alejandro, J. (2010). *Journalism in the Age of Social Media*. Reuters Institute Fellowship Paper, University of Oxford.

Allan, S. (2005). 'New on the web. The emerging forms and practice of online journalism'. In Allan, S. (ed.) *Journalism: Critical Issues*. Berkshire: Open University Press, pp. 67-81.

Allan, S. (2006). *Online News*. Maidenhead: Open University Press.

Anderson, C., Bell, E. and Shirky, C. (2012). *Post-Industrial Journalism: Adapting to the Present*. Tow Centre for Digital Journalism, Columbia University.

Atton, C. (2009). 'Why Alternative Journalism Matters'. *Journalism* 10(3): 283-285.

Bahcall, S. (2019). ). *How to Nurture the Crazy Ideas That Win Wars, Cure Diseases, and Transform Industries*. New York: St. Martin's Press.

Baker, E. (1994). *Advertising and a Democratic Press*. Princeton: Princeton University Press.

Bardoel, J. (1996). 'Beyond Journalism: A Profession between Information Society and Civil Society'. *Journal of Communication* 11(3): 283-302.

Bardoel, J. and Deuze, M. (2001). 'Network Journalism: Converging Competencies of Old and New Media Professionals'. *Australian Journalism Review* 23(2): 91-103.

Barnhurst, K.G. (2011). 'The Problem of Modern Time in American Journalism'. *KronoScope* 11(1-2): 98-123.

Barnhurst, K.G. (2013). 'Trust me I am an innovative journalist and other fictions'. In M. Broersma and C. Peters (eds.) *Rethinking Journalism: Trust and Participation in a Transformed News Landscape*. London: Routledge, pp. 210-220.

Barnhurst, K.G. and Nerone, J. (2003). 'US Newspaper Types, The Newsroom, and the Division of Labor, 1750-2000'. *Journalism Studies* 4(4): 435-449.

Bauman, Z. (2000). *Liquid Modernity*. Cambridge: Polity.

Baym, N.K. (2015). 'Connect With Your Audience! The Relational Labor of Connection'. *The Communication Review* 18: 14-22.

Beckett, C. (2008). *SuperMedia: Saving Journalism So It Can Save the World*. Malden, MA: Blackwell.

Beckett, C. (2012). *WikiLeaks: News in The Networked Era*. Cambridge: Polity Press.

Beckett, C. and Mansell, R. (2008). 'Crossing Boundaries: New Media and Networked Journalism'. *Communication, Culture & Critique* 1(1): 92-104.

Bell, D. (1973). *The Coming of Post-industrial Society: Venture in Social Forecasting*. New York: Basic Books.

Bell, M. (1998). 'The Journalism of Attachment'. In M. Kieran (ed.) *Media Ethics*. New York: Routledge, pp. 15-22.

Benkler, Y. (2006). *The Wealth of Networks: How Social Production Transforms Markets and Freedom*. New Haven/London: Yale University Press.

Berger, A.A. (1998). *Media Research Techniques*. Thousand Oaks: SAGE.

Berger, A.A. (2011). *Media and Communication Research Methods: An Introduction to Qualitative and Quantitative Approaches*. Thousand Oaks: SAGE.

Berkowitz, D. (1997). *Social Meanings of News: A Text Reader*. London: SAGE.

Bernays, E.L. (2004). *Crystallizing Public Opinion*. New York: Kessinger.

Bernays, E.L. (1972). *Propaganda*. Port Washington: Kennikat Press.

Boczkowski, P.J. (2002). 'The development and Use of Online Newspapers: What Research Tells Us and What We Might Want to Know'. In L.A. Lievrouw and S. Livingstone (eds.) *Handbook of New Media: Social Shaping and Consequences of ICTs*. London: SAGE, pp. 270-286.

Boczkowski, P.J. (2004). 'The Process of Adopting Multimedia and Interactivity in Three Online Newsrooms'. *Journal of Communication* 54(2): 197-213.

Boczkowski, P.J. (2004a). *Digitizing the News: Innovation in Online Newspapers*. Cambridge: MIT Press.

Boczkowski, P.J. (2004b). 'The Mutual Shaping of Technology and Society in Videotex Newspapers: Beyond the Diffusion and Social Shaping Perspectives'. *Information Society* 20(4): 255-267.

Boczkowski, P.J. (2009). 'Rethinking Hard and Soft News Production: From Common Ground to Divergent Paths'. *Journal of Communication* 59(1): 98-116.

Boczkowski, P.J. and Ferris, A. (2005). 'Multiple Media, Convergent Processes, and Divergent Products: Organization Innovation in Digital Media Production at a European Firm'. *Annals of the American Academy of Political and Social Science* 597(1): 32-47.

Boczkowski, P.J. and Mitchelstein, E. (2009). *Between Tradition and Change: A Review of Recent Research on Online News Production*. Thousand Oaks: SAGE.

Briggs, A. and Burke, P. (2005). *A Social History of the Media: From Gutenberg to the Internet*. 2nd ed. Cambridge/Malden, MA: Polity Press.

Broersma, M. (2007). 'Form, Style and Journalistic Strategies. An Introduction'.

In M. Broersma (ed.) *Form and Style in Journalism: European Newspapers and the Representation of News, 1880-2005.* Leuven: Peeters, pp. IX-XXIX.

Broersma, M. and Peters, C. (2013). *Rethinking Journalism: Trust and Participation in a Transformed News Landscape.* London: Routledge.

Bruns, A. (2008). 'The Active Audience: Transforming Journalism from Gatekeeping go Gatewatching'. In C.A. Paterson and D. Domingo (eds.) *Making Online News: The Ethnography of New Media Production.* New York: Peter Lang, pp. 171-184.

Calabrese, A. (1999). 'The Information Age According to Manuel Castells'. *Journal of Communication Summer,* 172-186.

Cantillon, R. (2001). *Essays on the Nature of Commerce in General.* Somerset: Transaction Publishers.

Carey, J.W. (1974). 'The Problem of Journalism History'. *Journalism History* 1(3): 5-27.

Castells, M. (1996). *The Rise of the Network Society.* Oxford: Blackwell.

Castells, M. (1999). 'Grassrooting the Space of Flows'. *Urban Geography* 20(4): 294-302.

Castells, M. (2000a). 'Materials for an Exploratory Theory of the Network Society'. *British Journal of Sociology* 51(1): 5-24.

Castells, M. (2000b). *End of Millenium. The Information Age: Economy, Society and Culture* (Vol. III). Oxford: Oxford University Press.

Castells, M. (2001). *The Internet Galaxy: Reflections on the Internet, Business, and Society.* Oxford: Oxford University Press.

Castells, M. and Ince, M. (2003). *Conversations with Manuel Castells.* Oxford: Polity Press.

Chapman, J. (2005). *Comparative Media History. An Introduction: 1789 to the Present.* Cambridge/Malden, MA: Polity Press.

Christensen, C.M. (2011). *The Innovator's Dilemma.* New York: First Harper Business.

Cicero, M.T., Rackham, H. and Sutton, E.W. (1967). *Cicero. De Oratore.* Cambridge: Harvard University Press.

Couldry, N. (2003). *Media Rituals: A Critical Approach.* London: Routledge.

Couldry, N. (2004). 'The Productive "Consumer" and the Dispersed "Citizen"'. *International Journal of Culture Studies* 7(1): 21-32.

Couldry, N. (2013). 'Why Media Ethics Still Matters'. In S. Ward (ed.) *Global Media Ethics: Problems and Perspective.* Malden: Wiley-Blackwell, pp. 13-29.

Couldry, N. (2016). 'Reconstructing Journalism's Public Rationale'. In C. Peters and M. Broersma (eds.) *Rethinking Journalism Again: Societal Role and Public Relevance in a Digital Age.* London: Routledge.

Couldry, N., Livingstone, S. and Markham, T. (2007). *Media Consumption and Public Engagement: Beyond the Presumption of Attention.* Hounmills: Palgrave Macmillan.

Cozzolino, A. and Giarratana, M. (2011). *Technological Change and Two-Sided Platforms: Evidence from the Italian Newspaper Industry*. Bocconi University, Milan.

Crosby, P.B. (1995). *Quality without Tears: The Art of Hassle-Free Management*. New York: McGraw-Hill.

Currah, A. (2009). *What's Happening to Our News*. Reuters Institute for the Study of Journalism, University of Oxford.

Dahlgren, P. (1996). 'Media Logic in Cyberspace: Repositioning Journalism and its Publics'. *The Public* 3(3): 59-72.

Davies, N. (2008). *Flat Earth News. An Award-Winning Reporter Exposes Falsehood, Distortion and Propaganda in the Global Media*. London: Chatto & Windus.

Deacon, D., Pickering, M., Golding, P. and Murdock, G. (1999). *Researching Communications: A Practical Guide to Methods in Media and Cultural Analysis*. London: Arnold.

Flather, H. (1977). *The Way of an Editor*. Cape Town: Purnell.

Garrison, B. (2001). 'Diffusion of Online Information Technologies in Newspaper Newsrooms'. *Journalism* 2(2): 221-239.

Gawer, A. and Cusumano, M.A. (2008). 'How companies become platform leaders'. *MIT Sloan Management Review* 49(2): 28-35.

Gentzkow, M. (2007). 'Valuing News Goods in a Model with Complementarity: Online Newspapers'. *American Economic Review* 97(3): 713-744.

Gerlitz, C. and Helmond, A. (2013). *The Like Economy: Social Buttons and the Data-Intensive Web*. University of Amsterdam, MIT Press.

Gilbert, C.G. (2005). 'Unbundling the Structure of Inertia: Resource versus Routine Rigidity'. *Academy of Management Journal* 48(5): 741-763.

Gillmor, D. (2006). *We the Media: Grassroots Journalism by the People, for the People*. Sebastopol, CA: O'Reilly.

Goodwin, T. (2018). *Digital Darwinism: Survival of the Fittest in the Age of Business Disruption*. London/New York: Kogan Page Limited.

Habermas, J. (1989). *The Structural Transformation of the Public Sphere: An Inquiry into a Category of Bourgeois Society*. Cambridge, MA: MIT Press.

Hamilton, J.T. (2004). *All the News That's Fit to Sell: How the Market Transforms Information into News*. Princeton, NJ: Princeton University Press.

Hartley, J. (2008). 'The Supremacy of Ignorance over Instruction and of Numbers over Knowledge: Journalism, Popular Culture, and the English Constitution'. *Journalism Studies* 9: 679-691.

Hatchen, W.A. (2001). *The Troubles of Journalism: A Critical Look at What's Right and Wrong With the Press*. 2nd ed. Mahwah, NJ/London: Lawrence Erlbaum Associates.

Healey, M. and Rawlinson, M. (1993). *Interviewing Business Owners and Managers: A Review of Methods and Techniques. Geoforum* 24(3): 339-355.

Heinrich, A. (2011). *Network Journalism, Journalistic Practice in Interactive Spheres.* London: Routledge.

Herbert, J. and Thurman, N. (2007). 'Paid Content Strategies for News Websites'. *Journalism Practice* 1(2): 208-226.

Holt, J. and Perren, A. (2009). *Media Industries: History, Theory, and Method.* Malden: Wiley-Blackwell.

Horkheimer, M. and Adorno, T.W. (1944). *Dialectic of Enlightenment.* New York: Continuum.

Jarvis, J. (2009). *What Would Google Do?* New York: Collins Business.

Jenkins, H. (1992). *Textual Poachers: Television Fans and Participatory Culture.* London: Routledge.

Jenkins, H. (2004). 'The Cultural Logic of Media Convergence'. *International Journal of Cultural Studies* 7(1): 33-43.

Jenkins, H. (2006). *Convergence Culture: Where Old and New Media Collide.* New York: New York University Press.

Keen, A. (2007). 'The Cult of the Amateur: How Today's Internet is Killing Our Culture'. New York: Currency.

Kern, S. (1983). *The Culture of Time and Space, 1880-1918.* Cambridge: Harvard University Press.

Kincaid, H. and Bright, M. (1957). 'Interviewing the Business Elite'. *American Journal of Sociology* 63(3): 304-311.

Kovach, B. and Rosenstiel, T. (1999). *Warp Speed: America in the Age of Mixed Media.* New York: Century Foundation Press.

Kovach, B. and Rosenstiel, T. (2001). *The Elements of Journalism: What Newspeople Should Know and the Public Should Expect.* New York: Crown/Archetype.

Kopper, G.G., Kolthoff, A. and Czepek, A. (2000). 'Research Review: Online Journalism – A Report on Current and Continuing Research and Major Questions in the International Discussion'. *Journalism Studies* 1(3): 499-512.

Kvale, S. (2006). 'Dominance Through Interviews and Dialogues'. *Qualitative Inquiry* 12(3): 480-500.

Lacy, S. (1992). 'The Financial Commitment Approach to News Media Competition'. *Journal of Media Economics* 5(2): 5-21.

Lee-Wright, P. and Phillips, A. (2011). 'Doing It All in the Multi-Skilled Universe'. In P. Lee-Wright, A. Phillips and T. Witschge (eds.) *Changing Journalism.* London: Routledge, pp. 63-80.

Lévy, P. (1997). *Collective Intelligence.* Cambridge: Perseus.

Levy, D. and Nielsen, K. (2010). *The Changing Business of Journalism and Its Implications for Democracy.* Oxford: Reuters Institute for the Study of Journalism, University of Oxford.

Lippman, W. (1999). 'Public Opinion'. In H. Tumber (ed.) *News: A Reader.* Oxford/New York: Oxford University Press.

Livingston, S. and Bennett, W.L. (2003). 'Gatekeeping, Indexing, and Live-

Event News: Is Technology Altering the Construction of News?'. *Political Communication* 20: 363-380.

Livingstone, S. (2004). 'The Challenge of Changing Audiences – Or, What is the Audience Researcher to Do in the Age of the Internet?'. *European Journal of Communication* 19(1): 75-86.

Luhmann, N. (1995). *Social Systems*. Stanford, CA: Stanford University Press.

McLuhan, M. (1962). *The Gutenberg Galaxy: The Making of Typographic Man*. Toronto: University of Toronto Press.

McLuhan, M. (1964). *Understanding Media: The Extensions of Man*. New York: McGraw-Hill.

McManus, J. (1994). *Market-Driven Journalism Let the Citizen Beware?* London: SAGE.

McNair, B. (2005). 'The Emerging Chaos of Global News Culture'. In S. Allan (ed.) *Journalism: Critical Issues*. Berkshire: Open University Press, pp. 151-163.

McNair, B. (2006). *Cultural Chaos: Journalism, News and Power in a Globalised World*. London/New York: Routledge.

McNair, B. (2013). 'Trust, Truth and Objectivity'. In M. Broersma and C. Peters (eds.) *Rethinking Journalism: Trust and Participation in a Transformed News Landscape*. London: Routledge.

Mejias, U. (2013). *Off the Network: Disrupting the Digital World*. Minneapolis: Minnesota University Press.

Mersey, R.D. (2010). *Can Journalism Be Saved? Rediscovering America's Appetite for News Santa Barbara*. Oxford: Praeger.

Miller, A. and Reynolds, A. (2014). *News Evolution or Revolution? The Future of Print Journalism in the Digital Age*. New York: Peter Lang.

Napoli, P. (2010). *Audience Evolution: New Technologies and the Transformation of Media Audiences*. New York: Columbia University Press.

Negroponte, N. (1995). *Being Digital*. New York: Knopf.

Nerone, J. and Barnhurst, K.G. (2001). 'Beyond Modernism – Digital Design, Americanization and Future of Newspaper Form'. *New Media and Society* 3(4): 467-482.

O'Sullivan, J. and Heinonen, A. (2008). 'Old Values, New Media: Journalism Role Perceptions in a Changing World'. *Journalism Practice* 2(3): 357-371.

Parolini, C. (1999). *The Value Net: A Tool for Competitive Strategy*. Chichester: Wiley.

Pavlik, J. (2000). 'The Impact of Technology on Journalism'. *Journalism Studies* 1(2): 229-237.

Pavlik. J. (2001). *Journalism and New Media*. New York: Columbia University Press.

Picard, R.G. (1998). 'Measuring and Interpreting Productivity of Journalists'. *Newspaper Research Journal* 19(4): 71-84.

Picard, R.G. (2004). 'Commercialism and Newspaper Quality'. *Newspaper Research Journal* 25(1): 54-65.

Plato, Emlyn-Jones, C.J. and Preddy, W. (2013). *Republic*. Cambridge, MA: Harvard University Press.

Plato and Jowett, B. (1983). *The Portable Plato: Protagoras, Symposium, Phaedo, and the Republic*. New York: Penguin Books.

Plato and Koolschijn, G. (1981). *Politeia*. Amsterdam: Athenaeum-Polak & Van Gennep.

Ryfe, D. (2012). *Can Journalism Survive? An Inside Look at American Newsrooms*. Cambridge: Polity Press.

Rosen, J. (1999). *What Are Journalists For?* New Haven, CT: Yale University Press.

Sànchez-Tabernero, A. (1998). 'Some Controversial Ideas about Media Quality'. In R.G. Picard (ed.) *Evolving Media Markets: Effects of Economic and Policy Changes*. Economic Research Foundation for Mass Communication: Turku School of Economics and Business Administration, pp. 120-141.

Sandel, M. (2013). *What Money Can't Buy: The Moral Limits of Markets*. London: Penguin.

Sashkin, M. and Kiser, K.J. (1993). *Putting Total Quality Management to Work*. San Francisco: Barrett-Kohler Publisher.

Schiller, D. (1999). *Digital Capitalism: Networking in the Global Market System*. Cambridge/London: MIT Press.

Schiller, H. (1984). 'New Information Technologies and Old Objectives'. *Science and Public Policy* 12: 382-383.

Schudson, M. (1978). *Discovering the News: A Social History of American Newspapers*. New York: Basic Books.

Schudson, M. (2003). *The Sociology of News*. New York: Norton.

Schudson, M. (2008). *Why Democracies Need an Unlovable Press*. Cambridge: Polity Press.

Schumpeter, J. (1934). 'Depressions'. In D. Brown et al (eds.) *Economics of the Recovery Program*. New York: McGraw-Hill.

Schumpeter, J.A. (1939). *Business Cycles: A Theoretical, Historical and Statistical Analysis of the Capitalist Process*. New York: McGraw-Hill.

Schumpeter, J. (1942). *Capitalism, Socialism, and Democracy*. New York: Harper & Bros.

Schumpeter, J. (1950). *Capitalism, Socialism, and Democracy*. London: Routledge Classics.

Scullard, H.H. (1981). *Festivals and Ceremonies of the Roman Republic*. Ithaca, NY: Cornell University Press.

Shapiro, C. and Varian, H.R. (1998). *Information Rules: A Strategic Guide to the Network Economy*. Boston: Harvard Business School Press.

Shirky, C. (2008). *Here Comes Everybody: The Power of Organizing without Organizations*. New York: Penguin.

Singer, J.B. (2003b). 'Who are these Guys? The Online Challenge to the Notion of Journalistic Professionalism'. *Journalism* 4(2): 139-163.

Singer, J.B. and Ashman, I. (2009). "'Comment is Free, but Facts are Sacred": User-generated Content and Ethical Constructs at the Guardian'. *Journal of Mass Media Ethics* 24(1): 3-21.

Skok, D., Christensen, C. and Allworth, J. (2012). *Breaking News: Be the Disruptor*. Nieman Foundation for Journalism, Harvard University School.

Stark, D. (2001). 'Ambiguous assets for uncertain environments: Heterarchy in post-socialist firms'. In P. DiMaggio (ed.) *The 21st Century Firm*. Princeton, NJ: Princeton University Press.

Stober, R. (2004). 'What Media Evolution Is: A Theoretical Approach to the History of New Media'. *European Journal of Communication* 19(4): 483-505.

Sunstein, C.R. (2001). *Republic.com 2.0*. Princeton, NJ/Oxford: Princeton University Press.

Taleb, N.N. (2007). *The Black Swan: The Impact of the Highly Improbable*. New York: Random House.

Taylor, R. (2000). 'Watching the Skies: Janus, Auspication, and the Shrine in the Roman Forum'. *Memoirs of the American Academy in Rome* 45: 1.

Thompson, J.B. (1995). *The Media and Modernity: A Social Theory of the Media*. Cambridge: Polity Press.

Thurman, N. (2008). 'Forums for Citizen Journalists? Adoption of User-Generated Content Initiatives by Online News Media'. *New Media and Society* (10)1: 139-157.

Turow, J. (1997). *Breaking up America: Advertisers and the New Media World*. Chicago, IL: University of Chicago Press.

Turow, J. (2005). 'Audience Construction Culture Production: Marketing Surveillance in the Digital Age'. *Annals of the American Academy of Political and Social Science* 597(1): 103-121.

Turow, J. (2011). *The Daily You: How the New Advertising Industry Is Defining Your Identity and Your Worth*. New Haven, CN: Yale University Press.

Usher, N. (2014). *Making News at the New York Times*. Ann Arbor, MI: University of Michigan Press.

Van Dijk, J. (2006). *The Network Society: Social Aspects of New Media*. 2nd ed. London/Thousand Oaks/New Delhi: SAGE.

Van Dijk, J. (2009). 'Users like you? Theorizing agency in user-generated content'. *Media, Culture & Society* 31(1): 41-58.

Vehkoo, J. (2010). *What is Quality Journalism and How Can It Be Saved*. Reuters Institute Fellowship Paper, University of Oxford.

Yoo, C. (2011). 'Modeling Audience Interactivity as the Gratification-Seeking Process in Online Newspaper'. *Communication Theory* 21: 67-89.

Zavoina, S. and Reichert, T. (2000). 'Media Convergence/Management Change: The Evolving Workflow for Visual Journalists'. *The Journal of Media Economics* 13(2): 143-151.

*Online sources*

Accenture (2016). Insight Highlights Communications Traditional Publishers Fight Back. [Viewed 20 June 2016]. Available from: https://www.accenture.com/us-en/insight-highlights-communications-traditional-publishers-fight-back

Batsell, J. (2015). For Online Publications, Data Is News. *NiemanReports*. Winter. Available from: https://niemanreports.org/articles/for-online-publications-data-is-news/

Bell, E. (2015). Hugh Cudlipp Lecture. *The Guardian*. 28 January. Available from: https://www.theguardian.com/media/2015/jan/28/emily-bells-2015-hugh-cudlipp-lecture-full-text

Bell, E. (2016). Facebook Is Eating the World. *Columbia Journalism Review*. 7 March. Available from: https://www.cjr.org/analysis/facebook_and_media.php

Blanding, M. (2015). The Value of Slow Journalism in the Age of Instant Information. *NiemanReports*. Summer. Available from: https://niemanreports.org/articles/the-value-of-slow-journalism-in-the-age-of-instant-information/

British Council (2021). How to Spot Fake News. [Viewed 26 July 2021]. Available from: https://learnenglish.britishcouncil.org/skills/reading/intermediate-b1/how-to-spot-fake-news.

Carlson, E. (2015). Hedrick Smith: "If all we deliver is bad news, we lose credibility". *NiemanReports*. 31 July. Available from: https://niemanreports.org/articles/hedrick-smith-if-all-we-deliver-is-bad-news-we-lose-credibility/

Colhoun, D. (2015). Who's Funding Women-Run Media? *Columbia Journalism Review*. 26 October. Available from: https://www.cjr.org/analysis/the_establishment.php

Costa, C.T. (2015). 6 Pillars of a Revenue-Generating Business Model for Digital Journalism. *INMA Keynote Blog*. 23 February. Available from: http://www.inma.org/blogs/keynote/post.cfm/6-pillars-of-a-revenue-generating-business-model-for-digital-journalism

Davis, N. (2011). Why The Economist Is Winning. *Business Insider*. 21 July. Available from: http://www.businessinsider.com/why-the-economist-is-winning-2011-7?IR=T

Doctor, K. (2010). Newspapers Find Themselves Confronted by Brand Management. *Newsonomics*. 31 August. Available from: http://newsonomics.com/newspapers-find-themselves-confronted-by-brand-management/

Doctor, K. (2012). The Newsonomics of Crossover. *Nieman Lab*. 1 March. Available from: https://www.niemanlab.org/2012/03/the-newsonomics-of-crossover/

Doctor, K. (2015). Newsonomics: Why Native Apps Still Matter in the Age of Distribution. *Nieman Lab*. 17 August. Available from: https://www.niemanlab.org/2015/08/newsonomics-why-native-apps-still-matter-in-the-age-of-distribution/

Garber, M. (2010). The Gutenberg Parenthesis. *Nieman Lab.* 7 April. Available from: https://www.niemanlab.org/2010/04/the-gutenberg-parenthesis-thomas-pettitt-on-parallels-between-the-pre-print-era-and-our-own-internet-age/

Garelli, S. (2016). Why You Will Probably Live Longer Than Most Big Companies. *IMD Business School.* December. Available from: https://www.imd.org/research-knowledge/articles/why-you-will-probably-live-longer-than-most-big-companies/

Gillmor, D. and Stearns, J. (2015). The Future of Journalism Will Not Look Like Its Past – And That Is a Good Thing. *The Guardian.* 9 September. Available from: https://www.theguardian.com/media-network/2015/sep/09/hyperlocal-community-journalism-report-investment

GoLocalProv News Team (2016). Reasons Why 2016 May Be the Most Chaotic Year Ever in Media. *GoLocalProv News.* 8 January. Available from: http://www.golocalprov.com/news/5-reasons-why-2016-may-be-the-most-chaotic-year-ever-in-media

Gourarie, C. (2015). Print Is the New 'New Media'. *Columbia Journalism Review.* 7 December. Available from: https://www.cjr.org/business_of_news/back_in_print.php

Greenslade, R. (2015). Global newspaper industry's business model undergoes 'seismic shift'. *The Guardian.* 2 June. Available from: https://www.theguardian.com/media/greenslade/2015/jun/02/global-newspaper-industrys-business-model-undergoes-seismic-shift

Haile, T. (2014). What You Think You Know About the Web Is Wrong. *Time.* 9 March. Available from: https://time.com/12933/what-you-think-you-know-about-the-web-is-wrong/

Haile, T. (2016). The Facebook Papers. *Recode.net.* 9 May. Available from: http://www.recode.net/2016/5/9/11610100/the-facebook-papers-part-1-the-great-unbundling

Hansen, E. (2015). Medium's Evan Hansen: "The Real Unit of Exchange Is … People". *NiemanReports.* Summer. Available from: https://niemanreports.org/articles/mediums-evan-hansen-the-real-unit-of-exchange-is-people/

Ifla.org. IFLA Resources. [Viewed 26 July 2021]. Available from: https://www.ifla.org/publications/node/11174

Ingram, M. (2012). Dick Costolo: Twitter Is a Reinvention of the Town Square—But With TV. *Bloomberg News.* 28 November. Available from: https://www.bloomberg.com/news/articles/2012-11-28/dick-costolo-twitter-is-a-reinvention-of-the-town-square-but-with-tv

Innovation Media Consulting (2018). 11 Business Models For Publishers. *Innovation.* 16 September. https://innovation.media/newswheel/11-business-models-for-publishers

Ipsos (2019). *Internet Security & Trust*. Centre for International Governance Innovation. [Viewed 26 July 2021]. Available from: https://www.cigionline.org/ sites/default/files/documents/2019%20CIGI-Ipsos%20Global%20Survey%20 -%20Part%203%20Social%20Media%2C%20Fake%20News%20%26%20Algorithms.pdf

Isaac, M. (2014). Amazon's Jeff Bezos Explains Why He Bought The Washington Post. *Bits (The New York Times)*. 2 December. Available from: https://bits.blogs. nytimes.com/2014/12/02/amazons-bezos-explains-why-he-bought-the-washington-post/

Jarvis, J. (2006). 'Networked Journalism'. *BuzzMachine*. 5 July. Available from: https://buzzmachine.com/2006/07/05/networked-journalism/

Jarvis, J. (2008). Defining Quality in Journalism. *Buzzmachine*. 27 April. Available from: https://buzzmachine.com/2008/04/27/defining-quality-in-journalism

Jolly, J. (2016). How Algorithms Decide the News You See. *Columbia Journalism Review*. 20 May. Available from: https://archives.cjr.org/news_literacy/algorithms_filter_bubble.php

Journalism Tools (2016). An Astronaut's Guide to News Disruption. *Medium*. 21 June. Available from: https://medium.com/thoughts-on-media/an-astronauts-guide-to-news-disruption-cce81cf6ddcc#.rffp4q3c6

Keller, M. (2016). How "Platforms as Publishers" Could Threaten Journalistic Ethics. *Medium*. 20 June. Available from: https://medium.com/@ mhkeller/how-platforms-as-publishers-could-threaten-journalistic-ethics-6995f7487ff1#.3lou33b3q

Kilman, L. (2015). 'New Business Models for Newspaper Printing Companies'. *Wan Ifra Press Releases*. 10 July. Available from: http://www.blog.wan-ifra.org/ press-releases/2015/10/07/just-published-new-business-models-for-newspaper-printing-companies

Kinsley, M. (2014). The Front Page 2.0. *Vanity Fair*. 10 April. Available from: https://www.vanityfair.com/culture/2014/05/newspaper-journalism-michael-kinsley

Koski, O. (2015). How Participatory Journalism Turns News Consumers into Collaborators. *Nieman Reports*. [Viewed 10 July 2016]. Available from: https:// niemanreports.org/articles/how-participatory-journalism-turns-news-consumers-into-collaborators/

Koski, O. (2015). How Participatory Journalism Turns News Consumers into Collaborators. *NiemanReports*. 17 November. Available from: https://niemanreports.org/articles/how-participatory-journalism-turns-news-consumers-into-collaborators/

LaFrance, A. (2016). Does Facebook Really Need Journalism? *The Atlantic*. 15 June. Available from: https://www.theatlantic.com/technology/archive/ 2016/06/facebook-ate-the-universe-bye-universe/486944/

Lecompte, C. (2015). Automation in the Newsroom. *NiemanReports*. 1 September. Available from: https://niemanreports.org/articles/automation-in-the-newsroom/

Lecompte, C. (2015). To Fight Ad Blocking, Build Better Ads. *NiemanReports*. 26 October. Available from: https://niemanreports.org/articles/to-fight-ad-blocking-build-better-ads/

Lokar, A. (2021). Riconoscere le fake news imparando a leggerle. *Linguisticamente*. 28 April. Available from: https://www.linguisticamente.org/riconoscere-le-fake-news-imparando-a-leggerle/

Lowery, W. (2015). Newsrooms Need to Engage if They Want to See Real Change. *NiemanReports*. Spring. Available from: https://niemanreports.org/articles/newsrooms-need-to-engage-if-they-want-to-see-real-change/

McKinsey & Company (2020). Building a Digital *New York Times*: CEO Mark Thompson. *McKinsey & Company*. 10 August. Available from: https://www.mckinsey.com/industries/technology-media-and-telecommunications/our-insights/building-a-digital-new-york-times-ceo-mark-thompson?cid=soc-web#

Mind Tools Content Team. How to Spot Real and Fake News: Critically Appraising Information. *Mind Tools*. [Viewed 26 July 2021]. Available from: https://www.mindtools.com/pages/article/fake-news.htm

Perry, M.J. (2014). Fortune 500 firms in 1955 vs. 2014; 88% are gone, and we're all better off because of that dynamic 'creative destruction.' *AEIdeas*. 18 August. Available from: https://www.aei.org/carpe-diem/fortune-500-firms-in-1955-vs-2014-89-are-gone-and-were-all-better-off-because-of-that-dynamic-creative-destruction/

Pew Research Center (2015). State of the News Media 2015. *Pewresearch.org*. 29 April. Available from: https://assets.pewresearch.org/wp-content/uploads/sites/ 13/2017/05/30142603/state-of-the-news-media-report-2015-final.pdf

Pew Research Center (2021). 'State of the News Media (Project)'. Available from: https://www.pewresearch.org/topic/news-habits-media/news-media-trends/state-of-the-news-media-project/htt

Quart, A. (2015). It's Only Money. *NiemanReports*. 25 March. Available from: https://niemanreports.org/articles/its-only-money/

Quinn, S. and Quinn-Allan, D. (2005). *The World-Wide Spread of Journalism Convergence*. School of Communication and Creative Arts, Deakin University. Refereed paper presented to the Journalism Education Conference, Griffith University, 29 November – 2 December 2005. Available from: https://dro.deakin.edu.au/eserv/DU:30005866/quinn-worldwidespread-2005.pdf

Regan, T. (2014). Technology Is Changing Journalism. *NiemanReports*. 15 December. Available from: https://niemanreports.org/articles/technology-is-changing- journalism/

Reid, A. (2015). 'Context is God': Why the Media Needs a Change in Focus. *Journalism*. 18 March. Available from: https://www.journalism.co.uk/news/-context-is-god-why-the-media-needs-a-change-in-focus/s2/a564479/

RISJ (2015). Editorial Analytics: News Organisations Embracing Analytics and Metrics, but Most Have Far to Go. *Reuters Institute.* 22 February. Available from: https://reutersinstitute.politics.ox.ac.uk/risj-review/editorial-analytics-news-organisations-embracing-analytics-and-metrics-most-have-far-go

Rosen, J. (2011). What I Think I Know About Journalism. *PressThink.* 26 April. Available from: https://pressthink.org/2011/04/what-i-think-i-know-about-journalism/

Rosenwald, M. (2016). The Digital Media Industry Needs to React to Ad Blockers ... Or Else. *Columbia Journalism Review.* September/October. Available from: https://www.cjr.org/business_of_news/will_ad_blockers_kill_the_digital_media_industry.php

Rusbridger, A. (2009). First Read: The Mutualized Future is Bright. *Columbia Journalism Review.* 19 October. Available from: https://www.cjr.org/reconstruction/the_mutualized_future_is_brigh.php

Starkman, D. (2011). Confidence Game. *Columbia Journalism Review.* November/December. Available from: https://archives.cjr.org/essay/confidence_game.php

Starkman, D. (2013). The Future Is Medieval. *Columbia Journalism Review.* 7 June. Available from: https://www.cjr.org/the_audit/the_future_is_medieval.php?page=all

Stray, J. (2015). A Brief Guide to Robot Reporting Tools. *NiemanReports.* Summer. Available from: https://niemanreports.org/articles/a-brief-guide-to-robot-reporting-tools/

Thompson, D. (2014). Time Inc. Has a Big Problem—So Does Digital Journalism. *The Atlantic.* 9 June. Available from: https://www.theatlantic.com/business/archive/2014/06/time-inc-has-a-big-problemso-does-digital-journalism/372460/

Vehkoo, J. (2010). What Is Quality Journalism And How It Can Be Saved. *Reuters Institute.* [Viewed 20 June 2016]. Available from: https://reutersinstitute.politics.ox.ac.uk/our-research/what-quality-journalism-and-how-can-it-be-saved

Vinciguerra, T. (2015). How Cartoons Helped Define The New Yorker. *NiemanReports.* 10 November. Available from: https://niemanreports.org/articles/how-cartoons-helped-define-the-new-yorker/

Viner, K. (2013). The Rise of the Reader: Journalism in the Age of the Open Web. *The Guardian.* 9 October. Available from: http://www.theguardian.com/commentisfree/2013/oct/09/the-rise-of-the-reader-katharine-viner-ansmith-lecture

Vosoughi, S., Roy, D. and Aral, S. (2017). *The Spread of True and False News Online.* MIT Initiative on the Digital Economy Research Brief. [Viewed 26 July 2021]. Available from: https://ide.mit.edu/sites/default/files/publications/2017%20IDE%20Research%20Brief%20False%20News.pdf

Walker, M. (2021). U.S. Newsroom Employment Has Fallen 26% since 2008. *Pew Research Center*. 13 July. Available from: https://www.pewresearch.org/fact-tank/2021/07/13/u-s-newsroom-employment-has-fallen-26-since-2008/

Wallach, O. (2021). How to Spot Fake News. *Visual Capitalist*. 10 February. Available from: https://www.visualcapitalist.com/how-to-spot-fake-news/

Weinberger, D. (2015). What APIs Can Do for News. *NiemanReports*. 13 July. Available from: https://niemanreports.org/articles/what-apis-can-do-for-news/

Wikimedia Foundation (2021). Janus. *Wikipedia*. Available from: https://en.wikipedia.org/wiki/Janus

Williams, O. (2015). The Guardian Changing Media Summit 2015: day one – as it happened. *The Guardian*. 18 March. Available from: https://www.theguardian.com/media-network/live/2015/mar/18/guardian-changing-media-summit-2015-day-one-live-blog

Williams, T. Be a Disruptor to Avoid Disruption. *The Economist*. Available from: https://execed.economist.com/blog/industry-trends/be-disruptor-avoid-disruption

Wolff, M. (2015). How Netflix Flipped the Script on Television's Disruption. *NiemanReports*. Spring. Available from: https://niemanreports.org/articles/how-netflix-flipped-the-script-on-televisions-disruption/

Woo, W. (2015). Using Network News to Tell Small Stories with Big Impacts. *NiemanReports*. 2 November. Available from: https://niemanreports.org/articles/using-network-news-to-tell-small-stories-with-big-impacts/

Ziemer, J. (2016). Making and Measuring News: Data and Algorithms in Journalism. *Blogs LSE*. 24 February. Available from: https://blogs.lse.ac.uk/polis/2016/02/24/making-and-measuring-news-data-and-algorithms-in-journalism/

Zuckerman, E. (2015). Ethan Zuckerman: "Journalistic Organizations … Need to Have a Civic Impact". *NiemanReports*. 12 November. Available from: https://niemanreports.org/articles/ethan-zuckerman-journalistic-organizations-need-to- have-a-civic-impact/

## Part II

Ahuja, G. and Lampert, C.M. (2001). 'Entrepreneurship in the Large Corporation: A Longitudinal Study of How Established Firms Create Breakthrough Inventions'. *Strategic Management Journal* 22(6/7): 521-543.

Bourke, J. (2016). *Which Two Heads are Better Than One? How Diverse Teams create Breakthrough Ideas and Make Smarter Decisions*. Sidney: Australian Institute of Company Directors.

Burckhardt, L.A. (1990). 'The Political Elite of the Roman Republic: Comments on Recent Discussion of the Concepts Nobilitas and Homo Novus'. *Historia* 39: 77-99.

Cucinelli, B. (2018). *Il sogno di Solomeo: la mia vita e l'idea del capitalismo umanistico*. Milan: Feltrinelli.

Dugan, J. (2005). *Making a New Man: Ciceronian Self-Fashioning in the Rhetorical Works*. Oxford: Oxford University Press.

Ekeh, O.L. and Ogidi, A.E. (2015). Intrapreneurship and productivity of companies'. *ARC Journal of Sustainable Development* 1(1): 34-44.

Ekingen, E., Ekemen, M.A., Yildiz, A. and Korkmazer, F. (2018). 'The Effect of Intrapreneurship and Organizational Factors on the Innovation Performance in Hospital'. *Revista de cercetare si interventie sociala* 62: 196-219.

Ferrarotti F. (2013). *La concreta utopia di Adriano Olivetti*. Bologna: EDB.

Gawke, J.C., Bakker, A.B. and Gorgievski, M.J. (2017). 'Employee intrapreneurship and work engagement: A latent change score approach'. *Journal of Vocational Behavior* 100: 88-100.

Isaacson, W. (2021). *Steve Jobs*. New York: Simon & Schuster.

Judge, T.A., Piccolo, R.F., Podsakoff, N.P., Shaw, J.C., & Rich, B.L. (2015). 'The relationship between pay and job satisfaction: A meta-analysis of the literature'. *Journal of Vocational Behavior* 77(2): 157-167.

Ochetto, V. (2015). *Adriano Olivetti: la biografia*. Rome: Edizioni di comunità.

Olivetti, A. (1965). *Mondo che nasce*. Rome: Edizioni di comunità.Pinchot III, G. (1985). *Intrapreneuring: Why You Don't Have to Leave the Corporation to Become an Entrepreneur*. Cambridge: Harper & Row.

Powell, R.R. (2004). *Wabi Sabi Simple*. Avon, MA: Adams Media.

Seneca, L.A. and Solinas, F. (2015). *Lettere Morali a Lucilio*. Milan: Mondadori.

Vitruvio, P. (2002). *Vitruvio De architectura*. Milan: V&P Università.

Wiseman, T.P. (1971). *New Men in the Roman Senate, 139 B.C.—A.D. 14*. Oxford: Oxford University Press.

*Online sources*

Andı, S., Nielsen, R.K. and Selva, M. (2020). 'Women and leadership in the news media 2020: Evidence from ten markets'. *Reuters Institute for the Study of Journalism*. 8 March. Available from: https://reutersinstitute.politics.ox.ac.uk/women-and-leadership-news-media-2020-evidence-ten-markets

Bourke, J. and Dillon, B. (2018). 'The diversity and inclusion revolution'. *Deloitte Review* 22. Available from: https://www2.deloitte.com/content/dam/insights/us/articles/4209_Diversity-and-inclusion-revolution/DI_Diversity-and-inclusion-revolution.pdf

Bratt, C., Abrams, D. and Swift, H.J. (2020). 'Supporting the old but neglecting the young? The two faces of ageism'. *Developmental Psychology* 56(5): 1029-1039. Available from: https://www.ncbi.nlm.nih.gov/pmc/articles/PMC7144460/

Bricco, P. (2018). 'Che cosa unisce Adriano Olivetti e Steve Jobs'. *Il Sole 24 ORE*. 10 July. Available from: https://www.ilsole24ore.com/art/che-cosa-unisce-adriano-olivetti-e-steve-jobs-AEqL3FIF

Business News Daily (2020. 'How to create a culture of intrapreneurship'. *Business News Daily*. 18 March. Available from: https://www.businessnewsdaily.com/5972-create-intrapreneurship-culture.html

Cable, D. (2020). 'What you should follow instead of your passion'. *Harvard Business Review*. 24 November. Available from: https://hbr.org/2020/11/what-you-should-follow-instead-of-your-passion

Carucci, R. (2020). 'Build a relationship with a senior leader you admire'. *Harvard Business Review*. 23 October. Available from: https://hbr.org/2020/10/build-a-relationship-with-a-senior-leader-you-admire

Chamorro-Premuzic, T. (2013). 'Does money really affect motivation? A review of the research'. *Harvard Business Review*. 10 April. Available from: https://hbr.org/2013/04/does-money-really-affect-motiv

Chamorro-Premuzic, T. (2020). 'Why you should become an "intrapreneur"'. *Harvard Business Review*. 26 March. Available from: https://hbr.org/2020/03/why-you-should-become-an-intrapreneur

Cherubini, F., Newman, N. and Nielsen, R.K. (2020). 'Changing newsrooms 2020: Addressing diversity and nurturing talent at a time of unprecedented change'. *Reuters Institute for the Study of Journalism*. 29 October. Available from: https://reutersinstitute.politics.ox.ac.uk/changing-newsrooms-2020-addressing-diversity-and-nurturing-talent-time-unprecedented-change

Colombo, P. (2021). 'Olivetti, l'occasione perduta'. *Sole 24Ore*. Podcast. Available from: https://stream24.ilsole24ore.com/podcasts/olivetti-l-occasione-perduta-AEkeq2C

Daykin, J. (2019). Intrapreneurship. *Forbes*. 8 January. Available from: https://www.forbes.com/sites/jordandaykin/2019/01/08/intrapreneurship/#5edae6374ea3

Deloitte Digital (2015). *Five Insights into Intrapreneurship*. Available from: https://www2.deloitte.com/content/dam/Deloitte/de/Documents/technology/Intrapreneurship_Whitepaper_English.pdf

DelPo, A. (2014). 'Your rights against age discrimination'. *nolo.com*. 15 October. Available from: https://www.nolo.com/legal-encyclopedia/rights-against-age-discrimination-29577.html

DePaul, K. (2020). 'What to say when you're reaching out to someone on LinkedIn'. *Harvard Business Review*. 2 November. Available from: https://hbr.org/2020/11/what-to-say-when-youre-reaching-out-to-someone-on-linkedin

Dixon-Fyle, S., Dolan, K., Hunt, V. and Prince, S. (2020). 'Diversity wins: How inclusion matters'. *McKinsey & Company*. 19 May. Available from: https://www.mckinsey.com/featured-insights/diversity-and-inclusion/diversity-wins-how-inclusion-matters

Dowling, S. (2013). 'Olivetti's typewriter: "The iMac of its day"'. *Bbc.com*. 2 April. Available from: http://www.bbc.com/future/story/20130402-typewriter-is-ipod-of-its-day

Edwards, P. (2019). 'How Leonardo da Vinci made a "satellite" map in 1502'. *Vox*. 11 April. Available from: https://www.vox.com/2019/4/11/18306214/leonardo-map-imola

Geena Davis Institute on Gender in Media (2020). Available from: https://seejane.org/

Glassdoor (2014). 'Two-Thirds of People Consider Diversity Important When Deciding Where to Work, Glassdoor Survey'. *Glassdoor.com*. Available from: https://www.glassdoor.com/about-us/twothirds-people-diversity-important-deciding-work-glassdoor-survey-2/

Glickman, J. (2020). When you're younger than the people you manage. *Harvard Business Review*. 24 December. Available from: https://hbr.org/2020/12/when-youre-younger-than-the-people-you-manage

Gosselin, P. and Tobin, A. (2018). 'Cutting "old heads" at IBM'. *ProPublica*. 22 March. Available from: https://features.propublica.org/ibm/ibm-age-discrimination-american-workers/

Granelli, A. (2014). 'Da Olivetti a Steve Jobs, la retorica torna in azienda'. *Linkiesta.it*. 18 July. Available from: http://www.linkiesta.it/it/article/2014/07/18/da-olivetti-a-steve-jobs-la-retorica-torna-in-azienda/22272/

Grasso, A. (2011). 'Olivetti e Jobs: due vite parallele'. *Corriere della Sera*. 23 June. Available from: http://www.corriere.it/spettacoli/11_giugno_23/grasso-olivetti-jobs-due-vite-parallele_f64b6090-9d57-11e0-b1a1-4623f252d3e7.shtml

Grieco, E. (2020). 'Fast facts about the newspaper industry's financial struggles as McClatchy files for bankruptcy'. *Pew Research Center*. 14 February. Available from: https://pewrsr.ch/2vBgw2M

Hamel, G. (1999). 'Bringing Silicon Valley inside'. *Harvard Business Review*. September-October. Available from: https://hbr.org/1999/09/bringing-silicon-valley-inside

Hillenbrand, P., Kiewell, D., Miller-Cheevers, R., Ostojic, I. and Springer, G. (2019). 'Traditional company, new businesses: The pairing that can ensure an incumbent's survival'. *McKinsey & Company*. 28 June. Available from: https://www.mckinsey.com/industries/oil-and-gas/our-insights/traditional-company-new-businesses-the-pairing-that-can-ensure-an-incumbents-survival

Holland, K. (2017). '3 Reasons Why Intrapreneurs and Entrepreneurs Play a Very Different Game'. *RocketSpace*. 2 February. Available from: https://www.rocketspace.com/corporate-innovation/three-reasons-why-intrapreneurs-and-entrepreneurs-play-a-very-different-game

Ibarra, H. (2019). 'A lack of sponsorship is keeping women from advancing into leadership'. *Harvard Business Review*. 19 June. Available from: https://hbr.

org/2019/08/a-lack-of-sponsorship-is-keeping-women-from-advancing-into-leadership

Ibarra, H. and von Bernuth, N. (2020). 'Want more diverse senior leadership? Sponsor junior talent'. *Harvard Business Review*. 9 October. Available from: https://hbr-org.cdn.ampproject.org/c/s/hbr.org/amp/2020/10/want-more-diverse-senior-leadership-sponsor-junior-talent

Kassova, L. (2021). 'The Missing Perspectives of Women in COVID-19 news TEDx talk'. *AKAS*. Available from: https://www.akas.london/article/the-missing-perspectives-of-women-in-covid-19-news-tedx-talk

Kueng, L. (2020). 'Hearts and Minds: Harnessing Leadership, Culture, and Talent to Really Go Digital'. *Reuters Institute for Journalism*. 12 November. Available from: https://reutersinstitute.politics.ox.ac.uk/hearts-and-minds-harnessing-leadership-culture-and-talent-really-go-digital

Lopp, M. (2013). 'Entropy crushers'. *Rands in Repose*. 15 July. Available from: https://randsinrepose.com/archives/entropy-crushers/

Lopp, M. (2014). 'Chaotic beautiful snowflakes'. *Rands in Repose*. 1 June. Available from: https://randsinrepose.com/archives/chaotic-beautiful-snowflakes/

Lorenzo, R. and Reeves, M. (2018). 'How and Where Diversity Drives Financial Performance'. *Harvard Business Review*. 30 January. Available from: https://hbr.org/2018/01/how-and-where-diversity-drives-financial-performance

Lorenzo, R., Voigt, N., Tsusaka, M., Krentz, M. and Abouzahr, K. (2018). 'How Diverse Leadership Teams Boost Innovation'. *Boston Consulting Group*. 23 January. Available from: https://www.bcg.com/publications/2018/how-diverse-leadership-teams-boost-innovation.aspx

Marzo Magno, A. (2011). 'Olivetti P101, quando gli italiani erano Steve Jobs'. Linkiesta.it. 8 October. Available from: http://www.linkiesta.it/it/article/2011/10/08/olivetti-p101-quando-gli-italiani-erano-steve-jobs/6174/

Molella, A. (2012). 'The Italian soul of Steve Jobs'. National Museum of American History. 24 January. Available from: http://americanhistory.si.edu/blog/2012/01/the-italian-soul-of-steve-jobs.html

Mondal, S. (2021). 'Diversity and Inclusion: A Complete Guide for HR Professionals'. *Ideal.com*. 21 May. Available from: https://ideal.com/diversity-and-inclusion/

Nese, M. (2019). 'Garibaldi e Meucci, un'amicizia nata a New York'. *Mondo Cultura*. 24 June. Available from: https://cultura.moondo.info/garibaldi-e-meucci-unamicizia-nata-a-new-york/

Nielsen, R.K., Selva, M. and Andı, S. (2020). 'Race and leadership in the news media 2020: Evidence from five markets'. *Reuters Institute for the Study of Journalism*. 16 July. Available from: https://reutersinstitute.politics.ox.ac.uk/race-and-leadership-news-media-2020-evidence-five-markets

North J.J. (2015). *Individual intrapreneurship in organisations: A new measure of intrapreneurial outcomes*. University of York. Available from: https://core.ac.uk/download/pdf/42606125.pdf

Palmer, M. (2020). 'You don't need an innovation lab. you need a strategy lab'. *Sifted*. 27 October. Available from: https://sifted.eu/articles/corporate-strategy-lab/

Perron, R. (2017). *The Value of Experience: Age Discrimination Against Older Workers Persists*. Aarp.org. Available from: https://doi.org/10.26419/res.00177.002

Pew Research Center (2021). 'Newspapers Fact Sheet'. 29 June. Available from: https://www.journalism.org/fact-sheet/newspapers/

Phillips, K. (2014). 'How Diversity Makes Us Smarter'. *Scientific American*. October. Available from: https://www.scientificamerican.com/article/how-diversity-makes-us-smarter/

Pinchot, G. III (2011). 'The Intrapreneur's Ten Commandments'. *The Pinchot Perspective*. 20 November. Available from: https://www.pinchot.com/2011/11/the-intrapreneurs-ten-commandments.html

Power, B. and Stanton, S. (2014). 'How to prioritize your innovation budget'. *Harvard Business Review*. 24 September. Available from: https://hbr.org/2014/09/how-to-prioritize-your-innovation-budget

Smith, C. and Turner, S. (2015). *The Radical Transformation of Diversity and Inclusion: The Millennial Influence*. Deloitte University. Available from: https://launchbox365.com/wp-content/uploads/2017/03/us-inclus-millennial-influence-120215.pdf

Sostrin, J. (2017). 'To be a great leader, you have to learn how to delegate well'. *Harvard Business Review*. 10 October. Available from: https://hbr.org/2017/10/to-be-a-great-leader-you-have-to-learn-how-to-delegate-well

Statista Research Department (2020). 'Topic: Newspaper industry UK'. *Statista*. 31 July. Available from: https://www.statista.com/topics/5932/newspaper-industry-uk/

Sullivan, M.R. (2013). 'Sottsass, Olivetti, and the continuing lure of the Typewriter'. *Sculptural Things*. Available from: https://sculpturalthings.com/2013/07/17/sottsass-olivetti-and-the-continuing-lure-of-the-typewriter/

Tett, G. (2021). 'The human factor – why data is not enough to understand the world'. *Financial Times*. 28 May. Available from: https://www.ft.com/content/4f00469c-75da-4e29-baf3-b7bec470732c

Thurman, N., Cornia, A. and Kunert, J. (2016). 'Journalists in the UK'. *Reuters Institute for the Study of Journalism*. Available from: https://reutersinstitute.politics.ox.ac.uk/our-research/journalists-uk

Tobitt, C. (2020). 'UK local newspaper closures: At least 265 titles gone since 2005, but pace of decline has slowed'. *Press Gazette*. 20 August. Available from: https://www.pressgazette.co.uk/uk-local-newspaper-closures-at-least-265-local-newspaper-titles-gone-since-2005-but-pace-of-decline-has-slowed/

Trupia, F. (2014). 'Olivetti e Jobs: parlare future'. *Huffington Post*. 14 November. Available from: http://www.huffingtonpost.it/flavia-trupia/olivetti-e-jobs-parlare-futuro_b_4271574.html

Turner, D. (2007). 'The Secret of Apple Design'. *MIT Technology Review*. 1 May. Available from: https://www.technologyreview.com/s/407782/the-secret-of-apple-design/

U.S. Equal Employment Opportunity Commission. *Age discrimination*. Available from: https://www.eeoc.gov/age-discrimination

Uviebinene, E. (2021). 'A successful career pivot starts with a student mindset'. *Financial Times*. 11 March. Available from: https://www.ft.com/content/76800ee9-6442-4c18-9615-68ac4ac41b61

Verganti, R. (2010). 'Having ideas versus having a vision'. *Harvard Business Review*. 1 March. Available from: https://hbr.org/2010/03/having-ideas-versus-having-a-vision

Verganti, R. (2010). 'How to sell an idea to your boss'. *Harvard Business Review*. 30 August. Available from: https://hbr.org/2010/08/how-to-sell-an-idea-to-your-bo

Waldman, E. (2020). 'Am I old enough to be taken seriously?' *Harvard Business Review*. 25 November. Available from: https://hbr.org/2020/11/gg-ascend-pub-11-11-how-old-is-old-enough

Wong, K. (2020). 'Diversity and Inclusion in the Workplace: Benefits and Challenges'. *engage*. 14 September. Available at: https://www.achievers.com/blog/diversity-and-inclusion/

Zapier Editorial Team (2020). 'Millennials are managers now'. *Zapier*. 10 March. Available from: https://zapier.com/blog/millennial-managers-report/

Zuliani, N. (2018). 'Uomo, macchina, sistema, civiltà. Olivetti più grande di Jobs'. *The Vision*. 16 July. Available from: https://thevision.com/cultura/olivetti-jobs/